METHUEN PLAYSCRIPTS

The Methuen Playscripts series exists
to extend the range of plays in print
by publishing work which is not yet
widely known but which has already
earned a place in the acting repertoire
of the modern theatre.

The Land of Palms
and Other Plays

Commissioned by the Dartington Arts Society, *The Land of Palms*
is a full length play set by an oasis in the North African desert which
involves a power struggle between a colony of idealistic drop-outs
and a splinter group of the French Foreign Legion. The other plays
in this volume are each one act and include *Liebestraum*, a twenty-
five minute comedy on the theme of wife swapping, *George Reborn*,
a twenty-minute comedy about lust on the Yorkshire moors, and a
selection of brief sketches created in 1970 and 1971 for Philip
Hedley's company at the Midlands Arts Centre. These short pieces
have begun to pass into the repertory of late-night and lunch-time
theatre and are likely to prove as popular with both professional
and amateur companies as David Cregan's earlier plays.

The Land of Palms

Liebestraum
George Reborn
The Problem
Jack in the Box
If You Don't Laugh You Cry

DAVID CREGAN

B 1

First published in Great Britain 1973
by Eyre Methuen Ltd
11 New Fetter Lane, London EC4P 4EE
Copyright ©1973 David Cregan
Songs for *The Land of Palms* and
the song for *Jack in the Box*
© 1973 Chrysalis Music Ltd

Set by Expression Typesetters
Printed in Great Britain by
Fletchers & Sons Ltd, Norwich

SBN 413 30730 1 Hardback
SBN 413 30740 9 Paperback

Contents

Author's Note

In chronological order, *Liebestraum* is the first of these plays. It was found by Philip Hedley, director of the Midlands Arts Centre Repertory Company, in late 1970, and was performed in several late-night shows there. The other short pieces, except *George Reborn*, were written specially for these shows in 1971, and so gave me the lucky chance to practise with this company's singular talent for performing actions and words consequently upon the thought that inspired them.

The Land of Palms is the next in order, and was commissioned by the Patrons Fund of the Dartington Arts Society at Dartington Hall. The Commission required an equal number of men and women in the cast, and also that the play be easily performable by amateurs. Although inspired by the space in the old cider press at Dartington, its first, and for me immensely happy performance was in the Barn Theatre.

George Reborn, chronologically the last, was commissioned by the BBC for their programme 'Full House'. This commission was for a very theatrical piece, and in fact experience shows the play to work better in the theatre than on television. An off-stage tape recorder easily replaces the orchestra.

Many thanks are due to many people for these plays, especially Sam Walters of The Richmond Fringe Theatre for two lively productions of *George*, and Rhys McConnochie for immaculate realizations of *The Land of Palms* and *The Problem*. The book really belongs to Philip Hedley, though, for working with him in 1971 got me out of a long dry spell and indirectly resulted in all the plays here except *Liebestraum*. To him it is dedicated with many thanks.

The Land of Palms

THE LAND OF PALMS was first presented at the Barn Theatre, Dartington, on 14 November 1972 with the following cast:

PAULA, a captain in the French Foreign Legion, aged about thirty or a little more, tall and very good looking in a commanding sort of way. — *Darlene Johnson*

ADA, a rather comfortable and round person of uncertain age. — *Jo Warne*

KATE, a stringy, slightly worn blonde of twenty-three. — *Angela Wallbank*

BOBBIE, a clear-eyed brunette of twenty-three, but younger looking than Kate. — *Sandra Shipley*

MOLES, a man of any age, with a moustache, and a rough appearance, despite great gentleness. Long hair, I suppose. — *Barrie Houghton*

LOUIE, a thoughtful intellectual of thirty-five. — *Roger Mutton*

JIM, a slight man, a private in the French Foreign Legion. Aged thirty-five. — *Peter Benson*

ROBERT, a tortured looking man, the same age as the above two men. Also a private in the French Foreign Legion. — *Nick Brimble*

Directed by Rhys McConnochie
Designed by David Fisher
Songs composed by Martin Duncan and Brian Protheroe

All the characters in this play are English.

The play is set on a bare white stage, and the action covers thirty-six hours.

Act One

A bare white stage. The voice of a girl in her early thirties can be heard off shouting orders. It is PAULA.

PAULA: Parade! Into file, left — turn! By the front, quick — march! Left, left, left right left.

(She keeps up the step. Enter PAULA, marching. She is a very attractive and tall girl in the uniform of a captain in the French Foreign Legion. Behind her come JIM and ROBERT, both privates, and both marching very smartly with rifles over their shoulders.)

Parade! Halt! Into line, left — turn!

(All three are now facing the audience. She walks slightly away from the men and begins to pace up and down, which she continues to do more or less throughout the scene.)

Order — arms! Stand at — ease! Stand — easy. You will have realized that there are very few of us left. I'm glad to say we are all British, but even we must face reality. The Foreign Legion was disbanded some years ago. The other nationals have gradually seen fit to admit it and have left. I can only believe that we, too, are now assumed to have deserted the fortress, to have abandoned our duties, and, in a phrase we all know to our cost, to have adapted to a new situation. Only this can account for the fact that no provisions have been received for something like eighteen months. Tonight therefore, we will march out alone into the desert to find our peace. Has anyone anything to say?

ROBERT (springing to attention): Sir!

PAULA: Yes Robert.

ROBERT: Death to the politicians.

PAULA: Yes Robert.

ROBERT: And death to my lifelong enemy, Louie Thompson of Reading.

PAULA: Oh?

ROBERT: I consumed my early years in hatred of Louie Thompson. To prevent that waste stretching through my life, and to cure myself of ulcers, I joined the Foreign Legion.

PAULA: I never knew that.

ROBERT: No one did. No one but we three ever shall.

(He stands at ease.)

PAULA: Has anyone else anything to say?

JIM (springing to attention): Sir!

PAULA: No, Jim.

JIM: Can't I say it one last time?

PAULA: I thought you'd got over it.

JIM: No sir.

ROBERT: Over what?

PAULA: No talking in the ranks! Very well. One last time.

JIM: I've loved your little sister Kate, sir, ever since I can remember, and I always will. You persuaded me to join the Legion, but I haven't forgotten her.

PAULA: She was thirteen at the time. It was very undignified.

JIM: She was so —

(He is lost for a word and seems to dream for a second.)

PAULA: Yes?

JIM: Blonde. Honey blonde. I thought if you touched her hair you would melt into a cloud of blonde honey feeling.

(After a moment he returns to the at ease position.)

PAULA: I also joined the Legion because of my sister Kate, among other things. She wouldn't do what she was advised to do. She walked around in bare feet. She kissed us all the time.

(She contemplates this. Then:)

Tonight then, after the Last Post has sounded, we will march off.

JIM: Which direction?

PAULA: There's an old Bedouin legend of an oasis deep in the desert where no one goes. We'll head south and either find it or leave our bones to bleach in the desert sun. Parade! Atten-tion! Slope — arms! Present — arms!

(The two men snap to the present, and PAULA salutes. JIM blows the Last Post through pursed lips. After he has finished, the salute holds for second.)

Slope — arms!

(The men slope arms and she drops the salute on 'slope'. PAULA begins singing quietly. The first seven lines of the song are, or are like, 'John Brown's Body', and the last seven are, or are like, the end of 'I've got Sixpence', where the words are 'No cares have I to grieve me'.)

We have fought in distant countries,
We have carried high the flag,
The Legion is our glory
And our glory doesn't drag.
We have marched across the continents
And not been known to sag,
We are steel in the Legion, we are steel.

(The men are by now singing, having begun by humming.)

We have steel in the blood,

We have steel in the bones,
We have kept your women safe
In the peace of home.
We have lifted up the high
And cut down the low.
We are steel in the Legion, we are steel.

Parade will advance into the desert in single file! Into file, left — turn!
By the front, quick march!

(Wheeling them if necessary and giving any additional orders that are required,
she follows them out, marching in time with them. They start the song again
and fade into the distance.

After a little while, a sound of Arab wailing comes from off-stage. A
group of apparent Bedouins come slowly out in a single line. Their faces
are covered with Bedouin handkerchieves and cannot be seen, and their
long robes hide the rest of them. It is they who are wailing. In fact, these
are MOLES, ADA, KATE, LOUIE and BOBBIE. These people are described
in the cast list.

The line goes into the middle of the stage and, still wailing, forms a
small circle. After a while it halts and faces inward. MOLES has meanwhile
detached himself from the line, and as far as possible has removed his Arab
costume to reveal a shambling, long-haired man with a long moustache.
He has a gentle manner, and a ready smile, though he has the figure and
gait of a bruiser. He is dressed in a very elegant kaftan and pale blue velvet
trousers. He addresses the audience, having waved the others to silence. They
squat.)

MOLES: They're contemplating. Isn't that nice? This oasis figures in an old
Bedouin legend. It lies deep in the desert and no one comes here. My name
is Moles. M-O-L-E-S. Moles. The oasis proper is just out there. Everyday we
come to this little sand dune, deep in the great immensity, and we come first
thing before breakfast and last thing before bed, and we contemplate, and
those Arab clothes help us to forget ourselves.

(He looks back at the group.)

They're so nice. (To audience.) Aren't they nice? My name's Moles. We're
preserving Life here. When everyone else is dead we'll be still here, growing
things, helping one another — sharing. (He smiles.) Did I tell you my name
was — yes, of course I did.

(He turns to the others.)

Good. Goody good good. Good. Breakfast. Just have them sing a few words,
Ada.

(He goes off. The others get up and turn to the audience and sing through
their handkerchieves.)

ALL (sing): There's no peace like long peace.
There's no life without peace.
There's no peace without a man.
Peace is all there is.

(MOLES returns during this with a camping tripod with a bowl on it, and carrying a shopping bag in which are vegetables. While he speaks, the others take off their Arab clothes. LOUIE is rather tidy and wears jeans and a long cardigan. He is thirty-five. KATE is a stringy and rather worn blonde of twenty-three and looks as if she has just given up cigarettes. She is in rather messy pale hippy clothes. BOBBIE is fresh, and although twenty-three, apparently, looks younger. ADA is a sensible round figure of uncertain age.)

MOLES (to the audience in a knowing way): Every morning at this time someone washes the vegetables for lunch. Isn't that so?

BOBBIE: Yes.

MOLES: Seems to be an occupation people like. Part of the basic rhythm of keeping house. Home, you know? Whose turn with the vegetables?

BOBBIE (taking LOUIE's hand): Ours.

MOLES (smiling): Aaah. Off we go then. We'll give a shout when breakfast is ready.

ADA: And come when you're called. It gets dry.

(BOBBIE and LOUIE are left. The others go out taking BOBBIE's and LOUIE's Arab clothes with them. LOUIE removes his hand from BOBBIE's and they go to the tripod and start to prepare vegetables from the bag.)

LOUIE (after a pause in which they work): I don't find Moles an easy name to say.

BOBBIE: You realize that's mere inhibition.

LOUIE (after some self-discipline): I realize that's mere inhibition.

BOBBIE (after a moment of self-analysis): I don't find it easy to say, either. Part of me blushes every time I do.

LOUIE: All of me blushes every time I do.

BOBBIE: It'll get easier. I found it hard to say Louie to begin with.

LOUIE: I don't see why.

BOBBIE: No, well, it's your name.

LOUIE: Are you being personal?

BOBBIE: To be absolutely honest, yes, I am.

LOUIE: It isn't hard to say Louis the Fourteenth, so why should it be hard to say Louie Thompson?

BOBBIE: I never met anyone called Louie before.

LOUIE: If you want to know –

BOBBIE (exploding): And you had a hell of a cheek finding it hard to say Moles, having a damn silly name like Louie yourself!

(There is silence while they go on with the vegetables.)

D'you want to slap my face?

LOUIE (another introspective moment): No.

BOBBIE: I know what you want to say next.

LOUIE: Good.

BOBBIE: You go ahead and say it, otherwise the resentment will bubble up inside you.

LOUIE: No, it won't.

BOBBIE: Yes, it will.

LOUIE: I have no resentment of any kind.

BOBBIE: I can hear it.

LOUIE: *You* have resentment, not me.

BOBBIE: Oh yes, *I* have resentment, resentment of what you want to say next.

LOUIE: Then you're the only one resenting things because I have absolutely no resentment at all.

BOBBIE: You do, and you're trying to be one up on me by behaving well.

LOUIE: I don't and I'm not.

BOBBIE: You think my name's a bloody silly name too, don't you.

LOUIE: Yes.

BOBBIE: Right. (She calms down.) We must be honest with each other, Louie.

LOUIE: I think you're name's bloody silly, but it isn't really bloody silly, I just think it's bloody silly.

BOBBIE: Good.

LOUIE: Your name is Bobbie, my name is Louie, and his name is Moles, and that's just fine.

BOBBIE: It's really very easy, isn't it.

LOUIE: Yes. (Silence.) No, but I'll try to find it easy.

(They work on for a little.)

BOBBIE: There's another thing I want to tell you before you resent it. I'm stupid.

LOUIE: I know.

(She looks at him sharply.)

It's all right, I don't resent it.

BOBBIE: I resent it. I resent your knowing it before I told you.

LOUIE: Do you resent my knowing you have a pretty face?

BOBBIE: That's different.

LOUIE: It's a more subjective judgment. Some people might not find your face pretty, but almost everyone would find you stupid.

BOBBIE: We have to respect each other, you know, if we're going to live here all our lives.

LOUIE: I respect you, Bobbie.

BOBBIE: I want to believe that.

LOUIE: Good.

BOBBIE (slightly desperate): Let's go and see the captain.

LOUIE: Ada.

BOBBIE: She's the captain.

LOUIE: I'm still at the stage where all of me blushes when I say that.

BOBBIE: None of me blushes at all. Isn't that strange?

LOUIE: Or stupid.

BOBBIE (desperate): Please!

(He looks startled.)

Oh please, Louie, take me! I'm stupid with a pretty face, but I've so much to give you and I couldn't possibly eat breakfast feeling like this.

LOUIE: Take you?

BOBBIE: Yes.

LOUIE: Does that mean —

BOBBIE: Yes.

LOUIE (thinks, then): Yes. Well, that seems more or less in order, I suppose. I'll take you, or give to you or whatever it is.

(They go off quickly.)

ADA (off): Breakfast!

(Silence. Then very faintly, and raggedly, the end of 'We Are Steel In The Legion, We Are Steel'. Then PAULA's voice.)

PAULA (off): Left, left, left, right left!

(PAULA marches in giving the step and still very spry. Behind her, staggering come JIM and ROBERT, marching as well as they can.)

Column! Halt! Into line, left-turn! (They face the audience.) Order — arms! Stand at — ease! Let us — pray!

(Instantly the two men wilt. PAULA shuts her eyes and lifts her face slightly.)

Lord God of Battles, who lookest into the hearts of men, we thank Thee for weighing us in the balance and not finding us wanting. Amen.

(The other two are asleep on their feet. PAULA looks at them and snaps loudly:)

Amen!

ROBERT AND JIM (waking smartly): Amen!

PAULA (looking at the tripod and vegetables): Evidence of an unexpected civil population.

ROBERT: Do we occupy them?

JIM: Or liberate them?

(ADA has entered and looks at the three in some surprise.)

ADA: Good morning.

PAULA: Ah, you're English.

ADA: I think we're probably beyond that sort of thing.

PAULA: Oh?

JIM: *Beyond* it?

ADA: Perhaps you'd better come and talk to someone. There *is* breakfast.

PAULA: Wait. (She draws her revolver.) I think I'd better investigate. You may fall out.

ADA: Don't be surprised if a couple turns up to do the vegetables. Funny about that wash basin. This way.

(ADA and PAULA go.)

JIM: I've a sinking feeling in my stomach that we're going to have relationships.

ROBERT: I've overcome my fear of those. I'm able to make friends now.

JIM: You haven't been able to practise much recently.

ROBERT: That's why I look forward to this. It'll be forced upon us.

JIM: For the rest of our lives, probably.

(Enter LOUIE and BOBBIE.)

ROBERT: We may well flower, Jim. Beautiful human blooms in the midst of the desert.

BOBBIE: Good morning.

(The two Legionnaires whip round and cock their rifles.)

Don't be afraid.

JIM: What?

BOBBIE: My name's Bobbie and his name's Louie. We've been making love.

(A look of horror is passing over ROBERT's face and he slowly raises his hand to point at LOUIE. At the same time, an expression of amazement passes over LOUIE's face. He seems uncertain where to put his hands, but raises them in a defensive sort of way.)

JIM: We're a detachment of the Foreign —

(He tails off as he sees the two men gazing at each other.)

BOBBIE: You seem to know each other.

ROBERT: Louie Thompson of Reading.

LOUIE: Robert the Hog.

(ROBERT turns to JIM and LOUIE turns to BOBBIE. They speak the next two speeches at the same time, initially to JIM and BOBBIE, but increasingly operatically all over the stage.)

ROBERT: This man has been my enemy ever since I can remember, causing me to grow up stunted, always in my dreams, driving me to be a Legionnaire of more than usual ferocity. His name is Louie Thompson of Reading, and I almost think I must be seeing things, except that he's so real, so bloody real, there in flesh and blood, Louie Thompson of Reading.

LOUIE (at the same time as the above): I've been this man's enemy ever since I can remember, and ever since I can remember he's been blaming me for all his troubles. His name is Robert the Hog, and I almost think I must be seeing things, except he's just as he always was, even as a little boy, whining and angry and dangerous.

(They face each other. ROBERT swings his rifle like a club and chases after LOUIE. ROBERT recites 'The Hound of Heaven', and LOUIE shouts 'Peace! Peace! Peace!' until they are held separate by the other two.)

ROBERT: I fled Him down the nights and down the days;
I fled Him down the arches of the years;
I fled Him down the labyrinthine ways
Of my own mind; and in the midst of tears
I hid from Him, and under running laughter.
Up vistaed hopes, I sped;
And shot, precipitated,
Adown Titanic glooms of chasmed fears,
From those strong feet that followed, followed after.

(Not all of the above quotation is necessary, but I give it in case it turns out to be. BOBBIE shouting 'Stop' manages to come between ROBERT and LOUIE while JIM manages to hold ROBERT's arm. JIM it is who finally holds him back and says over all the noise:)

JIM: This isn't making friends, Robert.

BOBBIE: Please realize you have come to paradise.

ROBERT: And there's the serpent!

(He raises his gun to shoot at LOUIE.)

BOBBIE (coming in the way): Oh for heaven's sake! He won't hurt you.

ROBERT: He hurts me by existing.

BOBBIE: Existence is a very beautiful thing. Life is a very beautiful thing.

ROBERT (gazes at her and then): Intellectuals! In the middle of the desert and what do you find but bloody intellectuals! For ten years I have tried to escape this man, God knows how I've tried, oh yes – (This to the skies.) – but You've crushed me! You've won!

LOUIE: Perhaps He wants us to be friends.

ROBERT: Don't mock me.

LOUIE: I never understood why we were enemies.

ROBERT: Look at our clothes. Isn't it obvious?

LOUIE: Perhaps if we used our reason, Robert, we could –

ROBERT: Reason? Oh God, Jim, take me away.

BOBBIE: That's cowardice. Since you've come to our community you must try to love each other. You must be honest with each other, open with each other. You must tell each other everything. We've just had a powerful demonstration of what can happen when you're totally honest, haven't we, Louie.

LOUIE: Not now.

BOBBIE: And if you're honest, Robert, you'll see that there's another meaning in coincidence besides the angry hand of fate. You've been given another chance, a chance in fact to coincide. To come together and forget your differences. Who says I'm stupid?

JIM (admiring): Not me.

BOBBIE: Be open, then, Robert, and relax. Love your neighbour as yourself.

ROBERT: You're a politician, aren't you.

BOBBIE: We've come here to forget politicians.

ROBERT: My ulcer's warning me that you should be avoided.

BOBBIE (taking his hand): There now.

(PAULA enters.)

PAULA: What's this?

ROBERT (withdrawing his hand): Louie Thompson of Reading.

LOUIE: Me.

PAULA: We find ourselves woven into a web of chance, fate and other metaphysical phenomena with which I have very little patience, but which, I regret, it is impossible to ignore. I am the elder of a family of two sisters. My name is Paula, and I have just had breakfast with my little sister, Kate –

JIM: What?

PAULA: Whom I haven't seen for ten years and who is approaching us from an oasis in the middle of the desert as if she were walking across Chislehurst Common as of old.

(KATE enters, a little awkwardly.)

JIM: Kate!

KATE: Jim!

JIM: It's a mirage.

(He faints.)

ROBERT (cocking his rifle): Don't anyone move.

PAULA (quietly): Parade.

> (ROBERT leaps to attention.)

> Parade, slope — arms.

> (He does so.)

> I don't want any ugly scenes with the natives, Robert. (To the others.) Please carry on as normal.

> (They all look awkward.)

KATE: This is a moment of joyful recognition.

PAULA: I see you still aren't wearing any shoes.

KATE: My feet seem to —

PAULA: You won't have any feet left if you don't wear shoes. Robert, accompany me please on a brief reconnaissance. I want to anticipate any more moments of joyful recognition before they catch us unawares. Into file at right turn! By the front, quick march! Left, left, left right left.

> (She marches out beside him, giving him any necessary orders.)

KATE (approaching JIM): Jim?

LOUIE: Shall we go or would you like us to help you through a difficult period?

KATE: Please stay. Jim? Are you all right?

JIM: Is it really you?

KATE: I'm still a virgin, Jim.

BOBBIE: I don't think it's wise to start a new relationship with a lie.

KATE: It's not a new relationship, and I'm still a virgin mentally.

JIM: I'm still a virgin actually.

KATE: Oh my poor unhappy Jim.

> (She cradles him in her lap.)

LOUIE: You've met before?

KATE: I first loved Jim when I was thirteen and he was twenty-five.

JIM: And then we parted.

KATE: And now I'm twenty three and he's thirty-five.

BOBBIE: Well good old fate. What a pity you missed out on the really green years, though.

LOUIE: I'm thirty-five. How old are you?

BOBBIE (chastened): Twenty-three.

KATE: When I was thirteen, I was interfered with and there was a fuss.

BOBBIE: Most people are interfered with some way or another.

JIM: I never was.

KATE: It was you interfered with me.

JIM: But I didn't.

KATE: We know that now. At the time everyone said you did, though, so I believed them. The fact is we fell in love. I used to travel back from school on the bus Jim conducted.

JIM: I used to let you pull my pinger.

KATE: A pinger is a machine conductors used to have round their necks to punch holes in —

BOBBIE: I know that.

KATE: It was a very innocent thing to let me do.

BOBBIE: If you have something on your mind, Kate, you tell us.

KATE: I loved Jim.

JIM: And I loved her. And one day I stroked her hair.

(Silence. KATE and JIM are happy.)

BOBBIE: In other words —

JIM: No.

KATE: Really?

JIM: Yes. I never wanted anything else.

KATE: Paula knew me better than that. Mother and Father knew me better than that. That's why they persuaded Jim to leave the country. They knew I'd wait for you if you went to prison, and they didn't like you. I did wait. I still am waiting.

LOUIE: There are still some vegetables left to wash.

(He beckons to BOBBIE.)

JIM: Don't go.

KATE: Why not? We're through the difficult bit.

JIM: We aren't married.

KATE: This is the desert, Jim.

BOBBIE: Marriage is an inhibiting institution that belongs to the so-called civilized world.

JIM (nervous): You mean you want me to seduce you?

BOBBIE: Isn't that typical of a soldier? To seduce someone is as bad as marrying them. Just make love.

JIM (frightened): In the Legion we have to sleep with our guns in our beds.

KATE: No, Jim. Not any more.

BOBBIE: You don't need guns any more at all.

JIM: I don't think Paula's going to agree about that.

LOUIE: That's true. You may have to make a decision.

BOBBIE: He will have to make a decision.

KATE: You bet he will.

(They all turn to the audience and sing.)

LOUIE: Love or duty
That is now the question.
Guns or beauty,
So it will divide.

ALL (joining in): Kate or Paula
They will be the rivals
A case of all or
Nothing to decide.

What a thing to face after so many years.
There will be undoubtedly very many tears.

Let's have breakfast
Let a little time pass
Let's have breakfast
And let things slide.

(They go off taking the tripod and vegetables with them. After a moment or two MOLES enters with a large paper parcel.)

MOLES (to audience): Now this is the oasis, well after breakfast, somewhere on towards lunch. I live here, behind those palms which you can't quite see, and behind those palms is the pool, which you can't quite see either. We all have our little spots to settle in. Now then. Here's a parcel. Goody. There's a jeep hidden in the dunes, so we can get provisions and things, and sometimes letters. My name's Moles (Big smile.) I've told you that.

(He squats down and begins to untie the knot on his parcel.)

MOLES (singing rather tunelessly): Oh my name is Moles.
Oh my name is Moles.
Oh my name is Moles.
Oh my name is Moles.

(While he sings PAULA comes in with her revolver drawn.)

PAULA: Are you in charge then, Moles?

(MOLES turns and smiles, then laughs.)

Are you?

MOLES: No one is.

PAULA: Put that parcel down, then.

(MOLES considers. He looks at her gun. He puts down the parcel and he stands up very obediently.)

Are you Mr Moles, or Moles someone?

MOLES: Just Moles.

PAULA: You realize we have to live together, your people and mine.

MOLES: Well that's just fine. Welcome.

PAULA: So you surrender.

MOLES: Surrender what?

PAULA: Everything.

MOLES: Well now —

PAULA: Stay still. I have the gun.

MOLES: Can you put it down?

PAULA: No.

MOLES: If we're going to live together we can't have guns, can we.

PAULA: We *have* guns. Why is the woman Ada called the captain?

MOLES: She was in the Girl Guides.

PAULA: You are the commander of this oasis, and Ada is your adjutant. Do you surrender to me?

MOLES (pityingly): Aah. I'd like to show you a better way.

PAULA: I'll shoot if necessary.

MOLES: All right.

(He stands and whistles to himself.)

PAULA: Aren't you going to say anything?

MOLES: Have you seen a psychiatrist?

PAULA: What?

MOLES: What did he say?

PAULA: Nothing. I'm normal. Will you or won't you admit defeat?

MOLES: What about a priest, have you seen one of those?

PAULA: I'm a regular communicant in the Church of England and I don't suffer fools gladly. Will you or won't you —

MOLES: You're a very attractive woman.

PAULA: And I'm in charge.

MOLES: You won't get Jim to shoot his girl, and if you shoot Bobbie she'll become a martyr — she's that sort — and Louie will outsmart Robert, and the presence of carrion will attract vultures, who will drop bits of it in the water supply like they always do, dirty things, so what about those as facts to consider?

ADA (off): Lunch is ready.

PAULA (without apparent loss of dignity): I'd like to start this conversation again.

MOLES (going to his parcel): Right.

PAULA: Leave it.

MOLES: Why?

PAULA: It might be a bomb.

MOLES: It's a hat.

PAULA: A hat?

MOLES: A hat.

PAULA: I don't believe you.

MOLES: All right.

(He whistles to himself.)

PAULA: I'm a woman.

MOLES: I believe that.

PAULA: And I know when men are playing silly games. That is not a hat.

MOLES: Isn't it?

PAULA: Is it?

MOLES: You're the one who knows things.

PAULA: I'm asking for your co-operation.

MOLES: Ah.

PAULA: Stand back! You've been defeated.

(Enter ADA with a glass and a plate of food.)

ADA: Lunchtime.

PAULA: Halt.

(The bean sprouts are a little overdone, but the lemon juice has kept very cool.)

ADA (as if not seeing): The bean sprouts are a little overdone, but the lemon juice has kept very cool.

PAULA: Stay where you are.

ADA (giving MOLES plate and glass): Shall I get you something?

PAULA: I said —

ADA: You can join us if you want.

PAULA: We're negotiating.

ADA: I'd put that down then, if I were you.

(She begins to move off.)

PAULA: Wait.

(She begins to sing in recitative to the audience:)

We have a problem here that must be obvious to you.
Which point of view is going to win?

ADA (not in recitative and to MOLES): It's her problem, not ours.

PAULA (recitative): I'm in the unhappy position of having said what I'm going to d

Namely use my gun,
But they don't respond so how can I begin?

(Changing to the introduction to a song.)

What a pretty problem,
What a parlous state.
There seems no solution
Which is im – medi – ate.
Oh – !

(She then sings the following music hall song. While she does so, unseen by
her, the other two look at each other in a puzzled way, shake their heads,
and go off.)

Who'll be the winner
Of the O – a – sis?
I wonder. I wonder.
Who'll sit at dinner
And say, 'Do this!'
I wonder, I wonder.
Someone'll surely come out top.
And rule all the others and make them hop.
It's the way of the world, and it will not stop.
Oh who'll be the winner –
Oh who'll be the winner –
Oh who'll be the winner –
I wonder!

(She turns with a big smile in the hope the others will have joined in but they
haven't. They aren't there. In great anger she raises her gun to fire at them.
Then she lowers it. Then, either to music or over it she goes on:)

Nothing is clear.
Nothing seems entirely right.
I must hold myself –
My honour –
Myself –
I must be bright.
Bright.
I shall not rush.
There is a way to be.
To be and not to alter.
I will win
And be myself.
I will be
And I will win.

(She sings 'Who'll be the winner' again and leaves. Enter BOBBIE, ADA,
LOUIE, JIM and KATE. MOLES also comes on and addresses the audience.
The others have a variety of deck chairs – ADA a sun bed – which they
set up while he is speaking. KATE alone does not.)

MOLES: And here we are, after lunch, siesta time at Ada's. There's Ada. And no sign of Captain Paula. Well, well, well.

(He goes to his parcel, squats on the floor and begins to undo the string on his parcel.)

ADA: Who's peeling the potatoes?

KATE (immediately): Me.

(She grabs JIM's hand as he is about to sit down.)

JIM (nervous): Oh!

MOLES: That's nice.

JIM (anxiously as he is dragged off): We're just going to peel potatoes, that's all.

(They are off and at once ROBERT's voice is heard.)

ROBERT: Jim!

JIM (off and as before): I'm just going to peel some potatoes.

(ROBERT enters carrying his rifle at the ready. He looks fierce but controlled. LOUIE watches him with some fear. He circles the stage and stops near LOUIE with some meaning. LOUIE gets nervously to his feet. They glare at one another with their various emotions.)

BOBBIE: Paula said no ugly scenes with the natives.

ROBERT: Who asked you to speak?

BOBBIE: The atmosphere.

(ROBERT paces on round. LOUIE sits. MOLES tears off a covering of paper from his parcel. ROBERT whips round.)

MOLES (not looking up): There's no need to worry, though unfortunately you will.

ROBERT (sarcastic): You're very clever, aren't you.

MOLES: Wise, more than clever. I'm about the wisest person we're likely to meet in the next fifty years. (He smiles.)

ADA (rather chattily): Are you on guard, Robert?

ROBERT: I'm observing.

ADA: Ah.

LOUIE: What are you obs-

ROBERT (turning on him): I thought you'd say —

LOUIE: Oh for God's —

ROBERT: I've had enough!

LOUIE: Christ!

(LOUIE's last word is squealed out as he takes cover behind his deck chair. For suddenly, ROBERT has his gun to his shoulder. Almost as suddenly

ADA is pushing him round by the barrel. BOBBIE has her hands to her face in terror. MOLES is still busy with his parcel. LOUIE mutters the 'Our Father'.)

ADA: Now, now, now, now, now, now, now.

(MOLES rips off another layer from his parcel. ROBERT whips round.)

Now.

ROBERT (calming down sullenly): He was going to insult the honour of the Legion.

(LOUIE returns to chair.)

BOBBIE: You're very hung up about the Legion, aren't you.

ROBERT: Democrat.

BOBBIE: That's a very facile thing to say.

ROBERT: I shan't say any more, don't worry.

ADA: That's right. You sit in Jim's chair over here.

(He does. ADA stands on tiptoe to look off where JIM and KATE have gone to.)

MOLES (humming to himself): I've got a hat.
I've got a hat.
I've got a hat.
I've got a hat.

(He tears off another layer of paper, and tackles a fresh knot. ROBERT winces slightly.)

ADA: They've got the potatoes.

MOLES: Aaah.

BOBBIE: What does facile mean exactly?

ROBERT: Don't you understand the words you use?

BOBBIE: Not always. Language is like that. It's a pretty blunt instrument for digging into the deeper recesses of the mind.

ROBERT: Some minds need a pretty blunt —

BOBBIE: That's another pretty facile thing to say!

ROBERT (cocking gun): Silence!

(He achieves it. Everyone looks modest.)

If Paula wants no ugly scenes with the natives the natives had better shut up.

(Enter KATE and JIM with the tripod and wash bowl and a small bag of potatoes. ADA and LOUIE exchange smiles. MOLES tears off another layer of paper and tackles a fresh knot.)

JIM (to ROBERT): Has something happened?

ROBERT (surly): No.

BOBBIE: We all *have* to be open with one another, otherwise we'll all be susceptible to traumas.

MOLES: True. True, true, true.

BOBBIE: And personally I feel it would be very nice if, after all these years, Jim and Kate settled down.

ROBERT: That isn't possible.

LOUIE: Indeed it isn't.

ADA: No.

ROBERT: What?

BOBBIE: What?

KATE: What?

LOUIE: Whatever happens, none of us should interfere.

ROBERT: Who's interfering?

LOUIE: I'm not.

ADA: Turn round Robert and look out over the empty space.

ROBERT: I might be knifed.

JIM: I'll see no one knifes you.

ADA: You'll find the empty space is very soothing. I always do.

ROBERT: All right, but you'll know, all of you, that if anyone talks about Jim and Kate settling down, the Legion will be in disagreement.

(ROBERT turns his chair round and sits, his rifle between his knees, staring ahead. BOBBIE opens her mouth to say something. LOUIE reaches out and claps his hand over it. MOLES tears off a fresh layer of paper.)

MOLES: Robert disagrees.
Robert disagrees.
Robert disagrees.
Robert –

ROBERT: Yes.

(MOLES goes on tackling the new knot.)

KATE: I want to settle down. Pretty quickly.

(ADA and LOUIE shut their eyes as if going to sleep. BOBBIE looks suspicious and puzzled.)

JIM: We have settled down. Here we are, doing the potatoes.

BOBBIE: We haven't travelled all the way out to this oasis just to –

ADA (eyes shut): Would you like to go for a walk, Bobbie?

BOBBIE: In the desert?

LOUIE (eyes shut): I'll take you.

ROBERT (definite): No.

BOBBIE: I was just being frank, that's all. The thought of those two settling down to sexless death in this oasis makes me dry up all over. Why did she leave Chislehurst?

LOUIE: I don't think it's any of your business.

BOBBIE: You know how *we* felt this morning.

LOUIE: No one forced that.

BOBBIE: No one's forcing this.

LOUIE: Good.

BOBBIE: Am I being aggressive?

LOUIE: You're being simple and uncomplicated, which is worse.

ADA: Do you believe in mixed marriages?

BOBBIE: Mixed marriages would prevent racial prejudice.

LOUIE (opening eyes): So they would, but they aren't always easy to manage.

BOBBIE (pointing at KATE and JIM): Oh – you mean –

    (MOLES tears off another layer of paper.)

ROBERT: That bloody parcel!

MOLES: Sorry.

    (All this time KATE and JIM have peeled away at potatoes.)

KATE: Well?

JIM: I've kept you in mind as an ideal, Kate.

KATE: I've kept you in mind as a goal.

JIM: Well, there you are. We don't want to risk being disappointed, do we.

ROBERT (who doesn't turn round for these remarks or his): No.

JIM: No.

KATE: I do. All other men have been nothing to me. I must know how it is with one who's everything. And after all, we can't spend all our lives in the desert without laying hands on each other.

JIM: I do love you.

KATE (eyes hungry): I'm boiling over for you.

MOLES (sentimentally): Aaah.

    (He tears off another wrapping of paper.)

    There's plenty of space for you to go in.

JIM: I read a book once, where it said the sand got all over things.

    (He points to a potato in KATE's hand.)

    Put that in the water or it'll go bad.

    (KATE drops it in the water and advances on him. He backs away from her.)

    The sand was very painful, it said in this book.

KATE: We've got rugs.

JIM: You never know with sand, though. And then snakes.

    (KATE gurgles a suggestive laugh.)

    Oh really!

KATE: Yes, really.

JIM: Then there's the call of duty.

ROBERT: Remember the Legion!

KATE: There are many duties, Jim, and you have one to the girl you set on fire so many years ago on the number nineteen bus.

JIM: I didn't realize what I'd started.

KATE: You will do soon. (She has forced him nearly off the stage and now grabs his hand.) With this hand, I thee wed.

(And she whips him off the stage. He makes a startled cry. ROBERT in anguish turns round. He sees they have gone and fires two shots into the air.)

JIM (off): I must go — (A squawk and then silence.)

ROBERT (standing up): I've done my duty. There've been no ugly scenes with the natives, mainly because I've interpreted that incident as the normal activity of an occupying army. At the same time I've fired a shot as a call for help.

(He looks off.)

Paula!

(No reply. ROBERT's fury is suddenly released.)

My God you're bloody lucky I haven't shot the lot of you! I've lost the only friend I ever had. Gone with a whore!

ADA: You could help me peel the potatoes if you felt lonely.

ROBERT: We thought this was paradise. I can't think how we came to make such a mistake.

(He goes out. LOUIE is relieved and ADA climbs on her sun bed to look off the way KATE and JIM went.)

BOBBIE: I'd like to know what all that was about.

ADA: Romeo and Juliet.

BOBBIE: Everyone was so political.

MOLES (very calm still with his parcel): Shall I put the kettle on?

BOBBIE: You weren't being honest and open, were you?

MOLES: I will. I'll put the kettle on.

(He goes out, leaving his parcel now only a cardboard box, but taking the paper so far undone.)

BOBBIE: You were lying, somehow.

LOUIE (enumerating on his fingers): I believe in peace. I do, I really do believe in peace. I believe in self-control. I do, I really do believe in self-control. I believe in honesty. Now do I? No I don't. Yes I do. No I don't. I haven't got honesty clear.

BOBBIE: We must be honest. It's the only hope.

LOUIE: You're stupid. We do agree on that.

BOBBIE (cross): And we respect each other.

LOUIE: And we have to remain alive. Death and peace are not necessarily synonymous.

BOBBIE: I can understand why he hated you, Louie Thompson.

LOUIE: Because he's stupid, too?

BOBBIE: Because you're smug.

ADA (getting down from the bed): They've finished.

BOBBIE: You peeping Tom!

ADA: We have to get Jim on to our side, don't we.

(Enter MOLES smiling.)

MOLES: I do believe they were enjoying it.

ADA: That's a relief.

BOBBIE (exploding): You mean that act of love out there has been a sordid political intrigue?

(ADA and LOUIE begin to speak.)

Has Kate sold her body just to suit the political expediency of Moles and Ada and Louie?

(ADA and LOUIE begin to speak.)

Just because you're scared of someone you drove demented when you were a boy, you sent that girl out there to give her best to that crummy Jim, just to get him on *our* side?

LOUIE: No.

ADA: They're very much in love, they said so. It happens if he joins us it'll make six against two.

BOBBIE: I thought we'd left that sort of thing behind.

ADA: We have, and now we shall all be at peace because of our two lovers.

BOBBIE: That isn't an honest remark.

(MOLES, who has returned to his parcel and is squatting as before, cross-legged, before it, pulls out a papal triple crown and puts it on majestically, saying as he does so.)

MOLES: Wowee!

(He sits for a second or two smiling. The others gaze at him.)

I'm the wisest person here. I'm the wisest person in the world as far as we're concerned. At least, until the rest of you catch up. It seems to me just the sort of hat I need.

BOBBIE: It's an out-dated symbol of religious strait-jacketing.

(He stands up.)

ADA: I don't think I'd wear it all the time.

MOLES: Oh?

ADA: You don't want to wear it out. I'll make tea over in the sunset.

(JIM and KATE enter quietly and return to the potatoes. No one seems to pay much attention as MOLES bursts into a jolly tune which does not finish:)

MOLES: I have a hat,
    A beautiful hat,
    A mystical hat
    That is holy at that.
    Oh what a hat —

(ADA crosses the stage, saying to the lovers as she passes:)

ADA: Too much sand?

(The lovers become slightly aloof and draw apart as she goes off.)

MOLES (turning to them): So. Consummatum est. It is done.

JIM: I wouldn't go quite so far as that.

KATE: *You* might. It's me who wouldn't go quite as far as that.

BOBBIE: I'm all for honesty but there are some things I can't bear to hear. This has been done so coldly and with such calculation.

KATE: It was the worst fumble I can remember.

JIM: Perhaps not quite how D.H.Lawrence described it.

KATE: You sounded as if it was for you.

JIM: Well it was O.K.

KATE: Heaven knows what you'll do when it comes out all bursting flowers and fireworks then.

JIM: I'd rather talk about the weather at the moment.

LOUIE: Not a topic of great variety in the desert.

JIM: Oh you! Get out!

MOLES: Children, children. These are lovers' quarrels.

(He makes an expansive arm gesture.)

Happy times.

KATE: I had more fun at school. And there's been a kind of gymnastic quality about one or two since then.

JIM: It wasn't my idea in the first place. Where's Robert?

LOUIE: If it hasn't worked, why not march off again?

JIM: I don't know whether it's worked or not, do I. You find out these things gradually.

LOUIE: Carry her picture with you into the desert and die there happy, with Robert.

MOLES: No, no, no. That'll never do. There's nearly murder in that suggestion. If at first we don't succeed —

JIM: Well all right, but not now.

MOLES (to the tune of the 'Peace' song): There's no love like an old love,
  There's no home without a love,
  There's no love without a man,
  Love is all there is.

(Speaking to the audience:)

Now we're going to have tea, facing the sunset.

(Singing to the same tune he goes off, followed by the others taking the chairs and things:)

Oh yes, oh yes,
Oh yes, oh yes,
Never say a word of no,
Yes is all there is.

(The lighting goes slightly pink. Onto the empty stage comes ROBERT with his gun, alone. He looks all round. Having established that he is alone, he stands his gun on its butt as if he has stuck it into the ground with its barrel sticking up into the air. He speaks not exactly to the audience but off the audience.)

ROBERT: Solus. So-litude. Soul is sol-us. Sol*us* is sol*ace*.

(Then he weeps and cries out:)

Louie Thompson! Just when I was absolutely safe, just when I'd revealed myself to those whom I could call my own, there was Louie Thompson, smirking – damned liberal thinker – smirking in my desert! Oh gun, there's only you and I left. Dear honest rifle. Good wood, stern steel, bullets clean and true, who have upheld so much, cleared away so many rabblesome diseases like the clean knife of the surgeon, only you and I know how it is to be bright. And I wasn't allowed to use you even when they took away Jim. No quarrelling with the natives. Whoever let the word atrocity into the language to haunt us hard-working soldiers? Even she couldn't let me use you on those trash, those – those *people.*

(Unseen to him PAULA enters, an open half bottle of whisky in her hand.)

Well then gun, dear old friend, we must be married you and I, in the final ceremony.

(PAULA drinks from the bottle.)

Robert the Hog will find his freedom with you.

(He puts his mouth over the barrel. Speaking as well as he can, he continues.)

Farewell, decaying world. Farewell political graft.
Farewell ungrateful life, Farewell the Legion.
Farewell, farewell, farewell, farewell.

PAULA: Fire!

ROBERT (standing up): Who said that?

(He turns and, seeing PAULA, snaps to attention. He salutes.)

Sir!

PAULA: Why aren't you on duty?

ROBERT: I was doing the honourable thing.

PAULA: You weren't. I watched for ages and you didn't pull the trigger. Why did you leave the others?

ROBERT: I fired for help and you didn't come.

PAULA: For help?

ROBERT: I felt deserted.

PAULA: This oasis is ours, those people are ours, their provisions and transport are ours, and I don't want them lost through incompetence.

(He looks longingly at the whisky.)

You should be infiltrating the enemy, like Jim.

ROBERT: You mean —

PAULA: Why aren't you out there with honest Bobbie?

ROBERT: She belongs to Louie Thompson.

PAULA: Say his name properly without quivering.

ROBERT: Louie Thompson.

PAULA: Again.

ROBERT: Louie Thompson.

PAULA: Louder.

ROBERT: Louie Thompson!

(He glances over his shoulder.)

PAULA: Go on.

ROBERT: I don't want him to come.

PAULA: You're scared.

ROBERT: I just don't want to have to control myself in front of him again.

(Note: Apart from the first drink and one other I have not indicated where PAULA drinks from the bottle, which she may do wherever it is found correct. It should be noted that she does not get drunk, at least not in the tipsy or incoherent meaning of the word.)

PAULA: Well then, you must infiltrate his girlfriend.

ROBERT: I couldn't.

PAULA: Why not?

ROBERT: There'd be great barriers of twisted adolescent life between us.

PAULA: Look on it as straightforward occupational practice.

(ROBERT shuts his eyes.)

Just this one thing, Robert, and then no one will ever ask you to adapt to a new situation again.

ROBERT: I never have adapted to a new situation.

PAULA: No. That's why we lost every colony we were ever sent to defend, and why, ultimately, none of us got any medals. There were always new situations to adapt to, and none of you could do it. This is our last chance Robert.

(She pours him a drink into the metal top of the bottle.)

Here the Legion. (They raise their vessels.)

ROBERT: The Legion.

PAULA: Freedom.

ROBERT: Freedom.

PAULA: Death.

ROBERT: Who's death?

PAULA: Drink up.

(They both drink.)

So. You will infiltrate.

ROBERT: I'll try.

PAULA: And so will I, even I, an officer, I will infiltrate like a common spy, and I will do it, as I can do it, better than any of you.

ROBERT: Paula.

PAULA: I will infiltrate their commanding officer.

ROBERT: He might interpret that as meaning he'd infiltrated you.

PAULA: But he won't have, I shall have done it and I shall have won.

(PAULA, eyes shut, head raised.)

Oh God of Battles, strengthen your soldier's heart. We are driven by you and we are driven for you, grant us this request. How can we put our foot on the anthill if we don't believe another foot hangs over us in the sky?

ROBERT: I want to kill Louie Thompson.

PAULA: Perhaps it could be justified.

ROBERT: You mean that?

PAULA: Perhaps.

ROBERT: You mean that I could put a bullet through his head simply and straightforwardly, in a perfectly open and honest way?

PAULA: Perhaps.

ROBERT: Oh! Oh my God! I feel ten years younger. He was always so right, always knew the answers, and yet in the exams he never beat me, because given time I was just as good as he was, so why did he lord it over me at dances and get the girls so that I was left holding his beer? Never once did either of us say a good word to each other, so why did we have to meet so often, since we lived so far apart, and then again here? Can I shoot him now?

PAULA: No.

ROBERT: You said —

PAULA: In the dark.

ROBERT: That's murder.

PAULA: No it isn't — Louie is a traitor. He's made love to your girl.

ROBERT (angry): She's not my girl!

PAULA: She will be — and we've known traitors in the Legion and we've dealt with them.

ROBERT: We left a revolver by the bedside.

PAULA: Some people never realized why it was there. Some people had to be shown what honour meant by having the barrel pressed against their temples, the trigger pressed against their wills, and their cowardice covered up by having the gun pressed into their dead hands as if they had, in fact, done what they should've done without having to be shown. This is such a case.

ROBERT: Ah.

PAULA: And your duty as a legionnaire is clear.

ROBERT: To do the honourable thing by Louie Thompson of Reading.

PAULA: Atten-tion! (He snaps into position. She shuts her eyes and raises her face.) God of our fathers, the way to honour is the way to freedom. Shine your light on that path so that Robert may follow it in high dignity and come to thine arms, a hero at the last.

(Silence. Faces shining. Enter BOBBIE with a cup of tea.)

BOBBIE: Tea?

(No reaction. Then —)

PAULA (looking down at the tea cup): For me?

BOBBIE: Moles sent it with his love.

PAULA (smiling but not taking it): Indeed. Thank you.

ROBERT: Amen.

PAULA: Amen. (She breaks from her position if she hasn't already.) Will you be honest with me, Bobbie?

BOBBIE: Of course.

PAULA: What do you think of Robert?

(He remains at attention.)

BOBBIE: He's a no good, hung-up, twisted and brutal fascist.

(ROBERT would like to reply.)

PAULA: Steady. (To BOBBIE.) He was twice recommended for the Croix de Guerre, but he was never given it. He has never had his capabilities confirmed to him. Milk and sugar?

BOBBIE: It's China.

PAULA: I should've known. He's a man, therefore, of wounded sensibility. Just now, for reasons that lie too deep for tears, he was about to take his own life with that gun.

ROBERT: I —

PAULA: Naturally he doesn't want just anyone to know that, but you are special, he says.

BOBBIE: Oh.

PAULA: Is that all you can say?

BOBBIE: I understand how he feels, not getting what he deserves.

PAULA: You've had the experience.

BOBBIE: I abandoned the competitive society because ultimately it was —

PAULA: Yes, it must've been.

BOBBIE: You don't know what I was going to say.

PAULA: You were going to say you were a failure. (Smiles.) Your honesty shines out of you.

BOBBIE: In certain terms, yes, I was a failure.

PAULA: Like Robert.

ROBERT: What?

PAULA: Give him my tea.

ROBERT: It's China.

PAULA: You'll like that.

ROBERT: I won't.

PAULA: You will.

BOBBIE: If he doesn't want it —

PAULA: He does. He's only sacrificing himself, as usual, by saying that he doesn't so one of us can have it.

BOBBIE (going to him): You're all disconnected, aren't you, and hung-up outside yourself.

ROBERT (checks with PAULA): Er — yes.

BOBBIE: And you're looking for a girl to help you.

(ROBERT, drinking his tea, nods. BOBBIE turns to PAULA.)

What about you?

PAULA (affronted by the idea but hiding it): We don't think of each other in that way.

BOBBIE: I thought officers had the welfare of their —

PAULA: In certain respects only.

BOBBIE: So you want me to do it?

PAULA: Shall I leave you?

BOBBIE (to ROBERT): It's rather difficult to have to say this, but I belong to Louie at the moment.

(ROBERT splutters into his tea.)

I knew you'd hate it.

ROBERT (giving the tea to PAULA): Take this.

BOBBIE: It really isn't any good, then, is it.

ROBERT: Standard occupational practice.

(He clamps her in a kiss. PAULA smiles.)

PAULA: Well! Young love.

(Enter ADA.)

Good afternoon. We're fraternizing.

ADA: You might encourage it among those of us who need it.

BOBBIE (breaks from the kiss for a moment): Help!

(ROBERT clamps her back again.)

ADA: It sounds more like rape.

PAULA: Oh, that isn't rape.

ADA: I don't suppose he's very good at rape.

(ROBERT lets go.)

ROBERT: Well? Who's better at it?

BOBBIE: He is, of course.

ROBERT: He's a traitor.

(He runs towards the gun.)

PAULA: No.

(He halts before the gun.)

ROBERT: But you said —

PAULA: Control yourself.

(He stands about disconsolately without his gun.)

BOBBIE: Excuse me. My tea's waiting.

(She goes out.)

ROBERT: Why must I control myself?

ADA: Rise above it, Robert. Smile.

(He looks at her in amazement.)

I used to be a primary school teacher. Would you like to talk to me?

PAULA: No.

ADA: I see. There's more tea if you want it.

> (She too goes out. She says to the audience as she does:)

> That one's mine.

ROBERT: I could've gone for him and done it then.

PAULA: Tonight, Robert. *Crime Passionnel* and execution of a traitor all in one. Jim! And don't bungle it.

ROBERT: I won't.

> (JIM comes in with his rifle.)

JIM: I want you to know that I like these people and I think we should treat them very well.

PAULA: Fall – in.

> (They do so, JIM talking the while.)

JIM: Robert'll do Louie some injury if we aren't careful.

PAULA: Parade. Stand at – ease.

JIM: I'm not sure how my marriage is going, exactly –

PAULA: Atten – tion.

JIM: But there's something rather nice about doing nothing all day. (He catches her eye.) Oh. I'm sorry.

PAULA: You will have noticed that we are now all part of a big happy family. There's still some slight dispute as to who is the head of that family, although I think we know who is. I think we know, too, whose home this is in the oasis; it is ours. (JIM is trying to interrupt.) Please.

JIM: I don't quite –

PAULA (a mild reproof): Jim.

> (He is silent.)

> We'll march out into the desert now to salute the colours as the sunlight fades, and then we'll take our oaths.

JIM: What oaths?

PAULA: Parade! Parade, slope arms! Into file, left – turn. By the front, quick – march.

> (They march out, she and ROBERT humming their song.
> There is the familiar wailing sound and MOLES comes in in his Arab costume. He doesn't have his mask up. BOBBIE, ADA, KATE, and LOUIE are filing in to sit in a circle, which they do, wailing quietly, as MOLES speaks. They are completely hidden by their outfits. The moonlight should somehow fall behind them so that we only see them in silhouette.)

MOLES (to audience): Here we are again, going out into the desert for our quiet time, before bed. We sit and we contemplate and we do our own thing. This is the desert, about half a mile from the oasis, and here it is, moonlight, and all of us sitting in the sand, our souls free, our bodies concealed, heigh ho.

(He joins them and they sit in silence. Then off stage can be heard the faint humming of the song. Then PAULA's voice.)

PAULA: Column, halt. Arabs. On your stomachs, down.

BOBBIE: It's them.

MOLES: Contemplate.

PAULA (off): On your stomachs, crawl.

JIM: I can't. The sand's getting up my tunic.

KATE: That's my boy.

LOUIE: Moles, Robert'll kill me in the darkness, I know he will.

MOLES: You keep saying that.

LOUIE: He tried before in Reading. Several times.

MOLES: He can hardly kill you if he doesn't recognize you.

ADA: Unless they kill us all.

(They all turn towards ADA.)

Well, they might.

MOLES: We are at peace, my children. Contemplate, and don't give Louie away.

ROBERT (off): They'll see us if we stand.

JIM (off): They'll know we're here. Sixth sense, Arabs.

(The three creep in on tiptoe, guns ready. They halt.)

JIM: I wouldn't mind being an Arab. If there was still an Arab Legion I'd -

PAULA: Sh.

(They advance.)

Salaam. We come in peace.

ADA: Salaam. Then go in peace.

PAULA: We live in the oasis and would like to know your intentions.

ADA: To sit in peace for an hour to two and then to disappear into the limitless waste.

PAULA: Do you know the white man at the oasis who has the jeep?

ADA: A man of great wisdom. We Arabs call him El Awrence the Second. You are lucky to serve him.

PAULA: I do not serve him.

MOLES: It is unwise to let great opportunities go by without seizing them.

PAULA: Do you serve him?

ADA: No.

MOLES: Yes.

ADA: The language of the desert is mysterious. Farewell.

PAULA: Farewell, brother.

ADA: The blessing of Allah go with you, brother.

PAULA: Sister.

ADA: Really.

(The three legionnaires move away.)

BOBBIE (too soon): Wow, that was close.

(The legionnaires whip round. MOLES begins wailing and the others follow suit.)

PAULA (very deliberately): Stop that noise.

(It stops.)

I'd be lucky to serve him would I? Shouldn't let the opportunity slip. There are some pretty naked admissions of intention in that. Stand up. Get in line.

(They do, in a line.)

Which is which?

(They all say their names at once.)

ROBERT: Which is Louie Thompson?

JIM: Don't be so obsessed, Robert.

ROBERT: Keep out of this. Louie Thompson is a traitor and must be punished.

(By now all except one figure have put up their hands. PAULA walks forward and pulls this figure forward.)

PAULA: Thompson, Louie, you are well aware of the charge of which you have been found guilty, namely, undermining the morale of half my command by causing both unreasonable hatred and jealousy. Since the Legion is always on active service, and you have so far professed yourself an ally of this company, this constitutes an act of treason while on duty, and is punishable only by death.

ADA (for it is she): Don't be so silly.

PAULA (with sudden fury): Where is he? Which of you is Louie Thompson?

(ADA falls back among them and they all jumble together and then line up again. PAULA chooses a figure, and roughly pulls it out.)

PAULA: Thompson, Louie – I don't need to repeat myself.

MOLES (for it is him): No indeed. No, no, no.

PAULA: What the hell are you playing at?

MOLES: And what the hell are you playing at with all this talk of shooting?

JIM: I simply won't have this. These people are my friends.

PAULA: Company!

JIM: No, I won't have Louie Thompson intimidated.

(He walks down the line.)

Louie? Louie, I'll defend you.

ROBERT: Shall I shoot him?

PAULA: We can't afford it.

ADA (detaching herself and taking ROBERT's arm): Robert, come with me to the wilder parts of the dunes and I'll explain some mysteries to you.

ROBERT: What?

ADA: How it is you get ulcers and what to do about it and things like that.

ROBERT (rather desperately): I'm going to shoot Louie Thompson.

ADA: Nonsense, you could get life imprisonment and prisons are notoriously bad at curing ulcers. Now I wonder if you know some friends of mine who used to live in Wantage. Was it Wantage or was it Abingdon, or which of those Thameside towns is it that has a marketplace with a tall clock tower in the middle with a gentlemen's convenience underneath it?

(They are off, ROBERT having cast despairing looks at PAULA who remains immobile.)

JIM (searching amid the robes): Kate?

LOUIE: I'm still alive. Let's get away quickly, and think.

BOBBIE: What shall we do?

LOUIE: I told you — think!

(LOUIE and BOBBIE exit.)

JIM: Kate?

KATE: What?

JIM: Ah! Get out of those clothes and let's go home and get some sleep like a properly married couple. (She follows him as he moves off, saying to PAULA): We could be very comfy here you know.

(They leave.)

MOLES (to PAULA): What a very attractive girl you are.

PAULA: Yes.

MOLES: I suppose — in the fortress — being the only girl —

(He stops.)

PAULA: The rough soldiery. Brutes. Nothing sensitive.

MOLES (sympathy): Aaah. I'm going over to the pool. I'd be happy if you joined me.

(He goes. She pulls out the whisky bottle, and turns to follow him, drinking as she goes.)

PAULA: For my men and for the Legion. I will be master in my own house!
   (She exits.)

Act Two

It is still moonlight but the moon must be fuller because there is more light on
the stage. MOLES comes on. He isn't wearing his Arab costume. It should be
noted that the others do wear their Arab costume, at least until morning comes,
but except where indicated they have their masks or veils down.

MOLES (to the audience): A soft answer turneth away wrath. Still night time,
   and just over there is my place, with the pool just behind it. She's a lovely
   girl, a lovely, lovely, lovely girl. (He pulls out the empty whisky bottle.)
   This is the only thing I don't understand about her. Is it because she only
   did it for some ulterior motive? I only did it for an ulterior motive, but I've
   almost forgotten what it was. Surely she didn't make herself drunk because
   – I mean I'm not repulsive. No. Not *repulsive*. Beware of introspection,
   Moles, especially out here where it could become a habit. Have a cold bath.
   There's a wise fellow.

   (He goes off. Enter ADA with her sun bed and some blankets. She is
   followed by ROBERT who still holds his gun suspiciously at the ready.)

ROBERT: I do not love Bobbie.

ADA: No.

ROBERT: That's what I'm saying, clearly and with conviction.

ADA: Yes.

ROBERT: She belongs to my hated enemy, that's the point.

ADA (opening her bed and indicating off): There. I live by this palm tree.
   (She lies down.)

ROBERT: And what's more, I'm very good at kissing.

ADA (allowing no feeling): Is that so.

ROBERT (pacing, rather): I could become sentimental, you know, Ada. I feel
   it in me.

   (ADA waits in hope.)

   D'you know what you did out there?

   (She doesn't, but barely likes to say.)

   You interrupted me at the climax of my life. You stopped the execution of
   Louie Thompson. And then you talked psychology to me, which, to an
   Englishman, is in very bad taste.

ADA: Is this you being sentimental?

ROBERT: No, of course it isn't. I think I'll leave you.

ADA: You're such a generous man, aren't you.

(He turns back in the act of leaving.)

Why else do you lavish everything you have on Louie Thompson. He has a second rate mind, second rate ideals, a thoroughly shoddy attitude to life — yet you give him all the honour due to a hero. Hatred, execution, and rape of his girl — is he worth it, I ask myself.

(She shakes her head.)

Yet there you are, you see, you're generous.

(ROBERT looks as if something has been revealed to him.)

Wait here. I'll be back in a minute.

(She goes out.)

ROBERT (to the audience): That's all true. I am generous. It is not seemly that the honourable traditions of enforced suicide that have grown up in lonely desert fortresses celebrated for their stern sense of devotion should culminate in you, Louie Thompson. How could I have thought that you, a worm-eaten intellectual, should have the honour of carrying to the home of the heroes the final bullet spent in execution of a traitor? It cannot be.

(ADA enters bearing the tripod and the washstand.)

ADA: In case we feel like a wash or anything.

ROBERT: And then your girl. Your trollopy, trumpery, rubber-lipped floosy. To be bedded by me, me of the Legion.

ADA (shaking head): No.

ROBERT: No.

ADA: What an idea. When did you first meet him?

ROBERT: When I was four and a half. We were at a party and he wouldn't join in. I understood because I didn't want to join in either, but I saw it as my duty nonetheless, and I did join in and he didn't. He didn't!

ADA: Poor Robert.

ROBERT: And the image of Louie Thompson sulking behind the sideboard, saying nothing, shaking his head at every suggestion from blindman's buff to mince pies, has lived with me ever since. Imagine how I felt, when, having passed the eleven-plus exam, I entered Reading Grammar School for Boys and found him in the desk behind me. In six months there were stigmata on my back where his eyes focussed on me. The doctor realized there was something wrong, and talked to me most kindly, but I couldn't tell him, could I, that I simply hated another boy. I mean — And that girl of his is a trollop.

ADA: Yes.

ROBERT: A trollop.

ADA: Yes. Go on.

ROBERT: The climax came one day on a family trip to the Thames at the Goring Gap. Oh Goring Gap! Oh Thames! How civilized art thou! A soft small break amid sedate hills, flattish, edged with trees, and breezy bits of open land where children can fly kites; the river flanked with chunky homes, green railway trains, and long glass-covered pleasure boats cruising in a well-dressed kind of way — oh gentlemen in blazers and hampers of cold chicken!

ADA: No trollops.

ROBERT: Never.

ADA: So.

ROBERT: Well — strangely enough, since you mention trollops, on this par-ticular day, just as we arrived at our favourite picnic place, a motor coach went past, a motor coach full of people singing vulgar songs. It's incon-ceivable to me that anyone can sing vulgar songs in the Goring Gap. It's worse than urinating in church — St Martins in the Fields, for example. You can't do it unless your soul's dead. Well, Louie Thompson hadn't anything to do with that at all, not directly. What he had to do with, what he *had* to do with, was the episode of the cowslip in the thermos flask: it happened that my father, who was a civil servant of a minor kind — er — a post office clerk — was very fond of butter. He used to have butter on everything. When he was a boy, it was said he buttered his cornflakes, though I always disputed that because I doubt if they had cornflakes when my father was a boy. However, the story is handed down, especially from the Scottish branch of the family, that butter was a staple diet of us all, as far back as the Massacre of Glencoe.

(By now he has gone off stage and can be heard chattering away to himself.)

On this particular occasion, it being high summer and the time when people reach their ultimate desires —

(Silence as he fades away. After a second or two, ADA shakes her head and says to the audience.)

ADA (to audience): How very deep we are.

(Enter LOUIE.)

LOUIE: Is that the episode of the cowslip in the thermos flask?

ADA: What happened?

LOUIE: I can't remember. And he always got so angry when he tried to tell me that he never finished. What's this for?

(He is looking at the wash basin and tripod.)

ADA: It's come to mean something rather special, hasn't it?

LOUIE: Some of them call you captain.

ADA (as if rather surprised at the fact): Yes.

LOUIE: Ada, I want to make a peace initiative to Robert.

ADA: I don't know whether he'll be cured in time.

LOUIE: In time for what?

ADA: Anything.

LOUIE: Should I make my peace initiative to Paula?

ADA: We might have to get rid of her.

LOUIE: Ada?

ADA: She's a tactician. She'll use whatever's available to get her own way. Robert's hatred of you is available to her. It might turn out to be you or her.

LOUIE (singing, to the audience): I want to live, I don't want to die. There's not much future for me in the sky.

(To ADA.)

Save me from death at the hands of a maniac
I want to live and I fear I shall die.

ADA: You want to live, and I want a man.
I want to have him as soon as I can.
Are these two problems remotely connected,
You wanting life, and me wanting man?

(As soon as this finishes, ROBERT's voice can be heard again and LOUIE quickly hides his face.)

ROBERT (entering): So, before we knew where we were, he was spreading butter on a bunch of grapes.

(Laughs in what a heavy man might call a light way. Then, seeing the masked LOUIE, he becomes suspicious. He tries to remain calm.)

Who is it?

LOUIE: Jim.

(As ROBERT doesn't believe this, he has great difficulty in remaining calm. He continues to stare at LOUIE while speaking, while LOUIE backs off the stage.)

ROBERT: As you can imagine, a bunch of grapes isn't a thing you can easily spread butter on because of the spherical shape. Gradually my father, who was a man of iron control but hot temper, began to go very red, and to shout vulgarisms which, until the advent of the coach party, had never been heard in the Goring Gap before.

(LOUIE has left.)

Who was that?

ADA: Would you like to peel some vegetables?

ROBERT: Why?

ADA (from her bed): I want a man, I want a man,
I want a, I want a, I want a man.
You need a lady like me to look after you

You need a lady and I need a man.

ROBERT (eyeing her and beginning to move away): After he'd used up all the butter, I was sent down to a squalid little grocer's shop to buy some more. The butter they were impertinent enough to offer me was of inferior quality to the butter my father had so far used, but since there was no other, we had to make do with it.

(He is now out of sight and earshot. ADA gazes off in some amazement at his non-reaction to her song.)

ADA: I wonder if I was rather too frank?

(At this moment KATE enters with a rug and JIM's tunic to the middle of the stage, and BOBBIE with another rug to the rear of the stage, thus, with ADA at the front, making three specific areas of the desert which are assumed to be invisible to each other. Cantering through them in pants and vest comes JIM, on a long run, lifting his knees rather high as he says:)

JIM: Left right left right left right left.

(He stops, facing the audience, and says:)

Love makes you feel very good, like vitamins.

(He finds himself near ADA's area and sees the wash basin and tripod.)

Ah. May I take this?

ADA: Do.

JIM (picking the tripod and basin up): Thank you. Good evening.

ADA: You can't force things the way they're not meant to go. Rest a while, Ada.

(JIM has cantered back up the stage and off. ROBERT comes on to BOBBIE's area, saying:)

ROBERT: My father only used Danish butter despite his unswerving loyalty to the Commonwealth.

(He halts, suddenly seeing BOBBIE who has watched him approach.)

BOBBIE: I want to be friends with you.

ROBERT: I said my father only used Danish –

BOBBIE: I want to be friends.

ROBERT: I said –

BOBBIE: I want –

ROBERT: Never! Ours is a dark relationship.

BOBBIE: Dark?

ROBERT: Very dark.

BOBBIE: You're ill, Robert, d'you know that.

ROBERT: I most certainly do not.

BOBBIE: You could be so lovely.

ROBERT: Don't plead with me. I cannot love you.

BOBBIE: I don't think you understand what I meant.

ROBERT: I positively cannot love you. You're ridiculous.

BOBBIE: *I'm* ridiculous? Why do you keep your boots so highly polished when there's no one here to see?

ROBERT: You're here.

BOBBIE: Oh. Thank you.

ROBERT: Thank you?

BOBBIE: For thinking of me.

ROBERT: I couldn't *wear* my boots if they were dirty. My father, as I was saying —

BOBBIE: Would you like to sleep with me?

> (ROBERT looks amazed.)

> I'm very foolish, but they do say — I mean — I have been told that I have my talents.

ROBERT: D'you know what you're saying?

BOBBIE: Charity is more than chastity, and I do have some feelings for you as a fellow human, and I don't see why —

ROBERT: Well, I have no feelings for *you* at all. You're a slut, and you're saying dirty things. I want you to know that I don't love you.

BOBBIE: You do.

ROBERT: I don't.

BOBBIE: Then why d'you go on about it?

ROBERT: Because really I do. No! I mean I don't. I don't even go on about it.

BOBBIE (very understanding): Robert you're being very foolish.

ROBERT: Now we have it.

BOBBIE: Come and sit down.

ROBERT: Seduction, you see.

BOBBIE: I want to help you.

ROBERT: I wouldn't make love to you if you lay down with no clothes on and begged me to.

BOBBIE: All right.

ROBERT (having waited in case she did): I wouldn't even kiss your hand if you held it out to me.

BOBBIE: Right.

ROBERT (again, after a pause): I wouldn't say I loved you if you threatened suicide.

BOBBIE: Robert, let's get things straight between us.

ROBERT: Certainly. The trouble with Commonwealth butter is that it doesn't spread with anything like the ease of the more liquid Danish, and my father's temper was very far from being improved by the situation that now faced him, so he grew angrier and angrier, even there in theGoring Gap.

(He is now off and indistinct.)

BOBBIE: Robert!

JIM (entering to KATE's area): Kate, I'm back!

KATE (getting up): Oh good. (They kiss.)

BOBBIE (to the audience): I have a duty to follow him and see he doesn't do anything he might regret.

(JIM had brought with him the washstand and the tripod. He has put it down and is starting to wash. BOBBIE goes out. KATE has coiled down to a sitting position on the rug.)

KATE: How d'you feel about me now.

JIM: I love you more than ever.

KATE: Do you understand me?

JIM: Tomorrow, Kate.

KATE: Why are you washing?

JIM: I don't like to go to bed dirty.

KATE: How much more of you are you going to wash?

JIM: Just my face and hands.

KATE: What the eye doesn't see, the heart doesn't grieve.

JIM: I don't think it's that.

KATE: What is it then?

JIM: Perhaps it is that. I don't know.

KATE: Are you a very unconscious man?

JIM: Wasn't all that out there satisfactory?

KATE: Yes, but these things have to be faced. Just because we had flowers and fireworks and minds blown apart doesn't stop me wanting to know why you only wash your face and hands. You don't even wash the back of your neck.

(After an uncertain second or two JIM begins to wash the back of his neck.)

KATE: You don't have to. I just wondered why you didn't.

JIM: It's dripping down on my back now.

KATE: Then why did you do it?

JIM: It seemed illogical to stop, once you mentioned it.

KATE: Why stop at the neck?

JIM: I want to go to bed, not have a bath.

KATE: Why didn't you say so?

JIM: I have said so.

KATE: Why bother to wash at all?

JIM: Because I don't like waking with a dirty face.

KATE: Why?

JIM (angry): Because it means there's so much to do before you have breakfast. Oh Kate. I'm so sorry.

KATE: Why?

JIM: What?

KATE: I annoyed you and you lost your temper.

JIM: I want us to be inseparable and cloudlike.

KATE: The whole thing about love is that there are two of you, not one.

JIM: But you join together to make one.

KATE: There's still a certain amount of individual skill needed, isn't there. That's what we've been all about all day. It's no good just sharing the desire.

JIM: I spent all night last night marching across the desert, all morning realizing I'd found my long lost girlfriend, and all afternoon making love to her. I'm very tired.

KATE: Don't you clean your teeth?

JIM: I've always hated cleaning my teeth.

KATE: It's not very nice having people in bed beside you with bad breath.

JIM: Do I have bad breath?

(He blows on his hand to reflect his breath to his nose.)

KATE: Do you always do that?

JIM: My breath is fine.

KATE: But in the morning —

JIM: Oh all right!

(He begins to clean his teeth.)

KATE: It isn't all right. You always do everything I suggest.

JIM: It worked very well out there.

KATE: Yes. Yes it did. A real row of dots. You could describe it all so far and then dot, dot, dot, all the organs turned to ice cream.

(She contemplates that.)

I wonder if you ought to wash —

JIM (interrupting): No. Enough is enough.

KATE: Well that's a relief. I thought you'd never disagree.

JIM: I'm probably a late developer.

(LOUIE enters to them, as they kiss, lightly.)

LOUIE: Has he been here?

KATE: Who?

LOUIE: I suppose to some people my position does seem unimportant. Has Robert been here looking for me to shoot?

JIM: I wonder if we aren't exaggerating all this rather.

LOUIE: I don't think that's what we're doing, no.

JIM: I lived for ten years with Robert and last night was the first time I heard your name.

LOUIE: He was letting it all fester.

JIM: You don't really understand him, do you.

LOUIE: No. Would you like to explain what he meant about shooting traitors out there in the desert?

JIM: He does get excited, certainly.

LOUIE: Yes. So in the interests of peace and quiet, don't tell him you've seen me.

(BOBBIE enters to them.)

BOBBIE: He's coming. Cover your faces.

(LOUIE and BOBBIE cover their faces.)

KATE: Jim thinks that —

LOUIE (harshly): Cover your faces!

(KATE does so. ROBERT enters to them.)

ROBERT: — and he drew himself up to his full height and shouted, 'Louie Thompson, you have put a cowslip in my thermos flask! Deny it if you can.'

(He realizes he is amid a group of people.)

Where's Ada?

JIM: Ada?

ROBERT: Just now you were with Ada, dressed in one of those things. I said, 'Who is it?' and you said, 'Jim'.

JIM: I've been running round the oasis all evening.

ROBERT (releasing the safety catch on his gun): Someone's being clever. Where's Paula?

JIM: With Moles.

ROBERT (whose eye has fallen on LOUIE): Who are you?

LOUIE: Er — I'm Moles.

JIM: But you're with — (Stops.)

LOUIE: No, I'm not. Obviously I'm not. I'm not Jim, I'm not Robert, I'm certainly not Louie. I must be Moles.

ROBERT: I don't believe you.

(Slowly he raises his rifle. JIM walks in front of him.)

JIM: I'm doing my ablutions, Robert, and to a legionnaire that's very private.

ROBERT (lowers his gun and glares at LOUIE): 'Louie Thompson', cried my father. 'You have put a cowslip in my thermos flask. Deny it if you can.' That was the moment of greatest revelation in my life. My own opinions were suddenly confirmed, and I felt a whole black universe rising up behind me, and focussing through me on that one disfiguring element in the whole of creation, Louie Thompson of Reading.

(He stands in silence.)

KATE (pointing off): Ada lives over there.

(He goes off.)

JIM: You've undone him. As we came to this oasis he said he'd learnt at last how to make friends.

LOUIE: It wasn't my fault.

JIM: I wonder.

(JIM and KATE begin to settle on the rug.)

BOBBIE: Why not try being open with him?

LOUIE: What about?

BOBBIE: I don't know.

JIM: It *is* your affair.

LOUIE: Therapy. I must tell Ada to keep him talking. You go back to your place and wait.

(BOBBIE and LOUIE go off. ADA struggles up off the bed.)

ADA: It's no use going to sleep. If I'm going to have him, I must find him.

(She goes off.)

We have to get him on our side, you understand.

(Enter MOLES.)

MOLES: I'm not really here at all, but I had to come and tell you what's happening at my place. Except I can't. I mean really, it's too remarkable. And not merely pleasure, oh no. The father of his people is making the homeland safe. I'm giving myself for my children. Why fight when you can settle things in other ways? Peace reigns. Marvellous.

(He dashes off. Enter ADA to JIM and KATE.)

ADA (calling): Robert!

(She sees the washstand and the tripod.)

Oh.

(She looks at KATE and JIM snuggled up together.)

Well, then I'll have it back. No use wasting it.

(She picks it up and goes out calling.)

Robert. Robert!

(LOUIE enters to ADA as BOBBIE enters to her own rug.)

LOUIE: You must keep him talking, Ada. Ada?

ROBERT (off-stage with cool menace): Ha ha ha ha ha.

(LOUIE turns to look off-stage. Is alarmed. Turns back and holds his hands up.)

LOUIE: Go on then, do it.

(Enter ROBERT, ready to fire from the waist.)

ROBERT: Ha ha ha ha ha.

LOUIE: Quickly. In the back.

ROBERT: Ha ha ha ha ha.

(He fires. Everyone sits up.)

LOUIE: Aaaah!

(But, as he examines himself, he realizes ROBERT has missed.)

BOBBIE: Louie!

KATE: Louie!

JIM: Louie!

ADA (off-stage): Moles!

LOUIE: You missed.

ROBERT: Yes!

MOLES (off-stage): No.

LOUIE (shouting in amazement): He missed!

ROBERT (amused, and very loud): Don't anybody move.

KATE (pushing the unwilling JIM who begins to crawl away): Go on.

BOBBIE (calling): Where are you?

LOUIE: Now what?

ROBERT:(shouting): I'll kill him properly if anybody moves. I've got him covered.

(JIM turns round and crawls back.)

ADA (off-stage desperately): Moles, you're needed.

MOLES (off-stage): Go away.

ADA (disgusted): Oh really, Moles.

LOUIE: Why did you miss?

(ROBERT listens, all is quiet.)

ROBERT: Paula said I should shoot you; Ada said I shouldn't — it was a compromise. Now I'm going to make up my own mind about it. First, that girl of yours is quite revolting.

(LOUIE mouths, not knowing what to say.)

Deny it.

LOUIE: She's not.

ROBERT: She is.

LOUIE: She is.

ROBERT: She's not.

(LOUIE is lost.)

ROBERT: I love her.

LOUIE: Oh?

ROBERT: Laugh. Go on.

LOUIE: Ha ha. No, that isn't right.

ROBERT: Louder.

LOUIE: I'm very *glad* you love her.

ROBERT: I warn you against trying to trick me, Louie.

LOUIE: But aren't you happy, Robert? Happy? Can't you feel things bubbling up nicely inside you?

ROBERT: She's the sort of girl I could've married, I know that.

LOUIE: Is that all?

ROBERT: What d'you mean, *all*?

LOUIE: I mean don't you feel − passion − I mean other worldliness?

ROBERT: I could've married her.

LOUIE: I see.

ROBERT: You don't believe it?

LOUIE: Yes, I do, I do believe it.

ROBERT (angry): You're so pious. I know I should've joined the Labour Party in the sixth form, and gone on Aldermaston marches, since it wasn't very far away, but you all smiled, you smiled so bloody much. You were always right. There was never any guts, never any individuality. You joined things.

LOUIE: I didn't really join things.

ROBERT: No. Really, you're like me, solitary. You betrayed me all the time. You made me very lonely, Louie.

LOUIE: You needn't be lonely here. Especially as you're in love.

ROBERT: You really think that?

LOUIE: I'm sure of it.

ROBERT: Of course I must be lonely here. Because you're wrong. Everything you do is wrong.

LOUIE: If only you could just put that gun down . . .

ROBERT: No. There's no solution.

(He cocks and raises the rifle.)

Here we go.

LOUIE: Can I say something first? One thing? About Bobbie?

(ROBERT lowers the gun.)

If you shoot me, Bobbie will be heart broken. Wrongly, perhaps, but she will be, and you, who love her to the point of marriage, will be torn in all directions like the hero of an opera. Paula will despise you for being torn like that, which will make things twice as bad, and the following phenomena will occur. One. You'll become inefficient and sloppy in appearance — people do. Two. You might find yourself wishing you'd never shot me. Three. In that case, you'd be haunted by fears and doubts, of all kinds — unlikely you may think, but heroes often are so haunted — Rigoletto, Othello, Macbeth — Four — You may even begin to see hallucinations, not uncommon in the desert.

ROBERT: I know what you're trying to do. You're trying to get round me.

LOUIE: Not at all.

ROBERT: Well, A. You're wrong and always have been. B. You're therefore not speaking the truth and so C. I shall shoot you.

LOUIE: You're quite right, I don't ever speak the truth, so shoot me and you'll be happy.

ROBERT (aiming from the shoulder again): You're trying to confuse me.

LOUIE: Yes.

ROBERT (suddenly lowering the gun): Say goodbye.

(He raises the gun.)

LOUIE: You haven't re-loaded.

ROBERT (lowering gun to look): What?

LOUIE: Heeeeeelp!

(He runs off and past ROBERT who turns and raises the gun. At once ADA appears where LOUIE ran off, holding the tripod and washbasin aloft.)

ADA: Halt!

(He lowers gun.)

Make love me to Robert.

ROBERT: Of all the bloody foul suggestions I ever heard.

(He runs off.)

ADA: So much for symbols.

(She hurls the tripod and basin off. It clatters. She goes off.)

KATE: What was that?

JIM: I don't know.

KATE (listening): It's gone very quiet.

JIM: Good.

(They snuggle down.)

KATE: Dear old Jim.

JIM (sleepily): I'm not old. I just like it when it's peaceful.

LOUIE (off, near BOBBIE's rug): Bobbie!

BOBBIE: Louie!

(LOUIE runs on to BOBBIE's rug.)

LOUIE: He's a raving maniac.

BOBBIE: Dear Louie.

LOUIE: Not now.

BOBBIE: Is maniac a useful word in this context, d'you think?

LOUIE: I think so, yes, in my position, yes, I find it useful. I'm being chased by a man who wants to shoot me for no reason that I know of. It helps me to understand things clearly to call him a maniac, which is what I think he is.

BOBBIE: He's just very disturbed.

LOUIE: Yes.

BOBBIE: We have to find the cause of that disturbance.

LOUIE: *I'm* the cause of that disturbance.

BOBBIE: Well, what is it you do?

LOUIE: I live. Where's he got to?

BOBBIE: Face it Louie. You must know why he hates you.

LOUIE: He hates me because he's been twisted. I don't know who twisted him, or who twisted the people who twisted them or whether he was conceived twisted or got twisted in pregnancy. All I know is, it happened.

BOBBIE: Don't you care?

LOUIE: Of course I care. I came to this oasis because I hate all that.

BOBBIE: But don't you care about him?

LOUIE: I also care about me and he is going to shoot me if he can.

BOBBIE: What shall we do?

LOUIE: There are times, quite often, when there's nothing you can do except the impossible, which is to behave reasonably. It hasn't so far been successful.

(There is a shot off-stage.)

Christ.

ADA (entering to her bed with a book): I hope he's shot Moles.

BOBBIE: He's shot someone.

LOUIE: Can you see who?

BOBBIE: No.

(They peer into the darkness.)

KATE (sitting up): Robert's shot Louie.

JIM (lying still): Don't be silly.

ADA: I wonder if he has shot Moles?

(MOLES nips on.)

MOLES (to the audience): I didn't hear anything. I doubt if I'll ever hear anything again.

(He rolls his eyes with pleasure and nips off. Suddenly BOBBIE and LOUIE mask up. ROBERT can be heard singing part of the 'Legionnaire's Song' as he comes on to BOBBIE's rug. He halts and gazes at the other two. Silence.)

ROBERT: I've shot him. I'm eased of a great bowel movement.

BOBBIE: Look –

ROBERT: I'm purged, and everything about me is in order.

BOBBIE: Robert, you have to know –

ROBERT: Paradise has arrived at last. (Looks as if he has unfulfilled expectations.) Paradise.

JIM (whispering): Shall I go?

KATE (whispering): Yes, and shoot him if he looks like being a nuisance.

(JIM begins to crawl off again.)

ROBERT: Do you feel paradise?

BOBBIE: No.

ROBERT: No. It's rather flat.

BOBBIE: Look, Robert, this is Bobbie speaking to you.

(JIM is now off.)

ROBERT: Bobbie. You were his girl.

BOBBIE: Yes.

ROBERT: I should feel guilty, shouldn't I.

BOBBIE: Guilt is not a concept that I –

ROBERT (looking up): Come on! I should feel guilty!

BOBBIE: You haven't killed him.

ROBERT: Yes I have. I couldn't miss him twice.

BOBBIE: But you haven't.

ROBERT (emphatic): I could not miss him twice. (Upwards.) Let me feel guilt. Please. And you (To BOBBIE.) prepare to forgive me. (To LOUIE.) Make her forgive me, Kate.

(He goes out.)

BOBBIE: Well, aren't you going to tell him?

LOUIE: I don't want to be shot again.

BOBBIE: He's going mad.

LOUIE: But I think he's ours. I wonder who he did shoot. Wait here.

(He goes off. Enter ROBERT to ADA.)

ROBERT: Ah, Ada.

ADA: Ah, Robert.

ROBERT: I've done it. I've restored my father's picnic.

ADA: Is it nice?

ROBERT: It's nothing. I'm hoping to feel a sense of guilt quite soon but it's taking time to penetrate.

(JIM is now crawling on to BOBBIE.)

JIM: Psst.

(BOBBIE jumps up.)

ADA: I wouldn't press it.

ROBERT: No?

BOBBIE: Jim!

JIM: Robert's shot Louie.

ROBERT: But I *must* feel guilty. I must feel something.

ADA: Couldn't you feel happy?

ROBERT: Don't be shallow.

(LOUIE runs on to ADA and ROBERT and at once masks up.)

Kate? Has Bobbie forgiven me?

(LOUIE shakes his head.)

Perhaps she will if I can get some steam into my repentance.

(Falls to his knees.)

Make me feel guilty!

ADA: Kate, just wait here while I find the body.

(She goes, to LOUIE's distress.)

BOBBIE (who has been having a whispered conversation with JIM): Perhaps he shot Ada.

JIM: Ada wouldn't let herself be shot, would she?

BOBBIE: Go and see.

(JIM looks annoyed.)

ROBERT: God of Our Fathers, let me know my crime. Let guilt flow through my veins in inky waves and let me feel repentance.

(JIM begins to crawl off, troubled with sand in his trousers.)

JIM: Bloody sand.

(LOUIE sits nervously on ADA's bed. ROBERT has his eyes shut tight. ADA enters to KATE.)

ADA: Kate? I left you with Robert.

KATE: I sent Jim after Robert to avenge Louie.

ADA: You sent that piffling little housewife to shoot my great romantic paranoiac?

KATE: We can't have him murdering everyone.

ADA: He's my man, very nearly. It's all very well for the rest of you, paired off here in the desert, but I'm on my own.

KATE: You don't want a murderer, do you?

ADA: Why not? Someone's got to have him.

(ROBERT is gazing at LOUIE's feet. He reaches for them and touches them. He then feels LOUIE's legs. LOUIE is frightened. They gaze at one another.)

ROBERT: The ghost of Louie Thompson.

LOUIE: Well, no, Robert, I *am* Louie Thompson. I don't quite know who you shot out there, but it wasn't me.

ROBERT: You are the ghost of Louie Thompson of Reading, my hated enemy, and oh God, and I can feel it coming, the guilt, it's coming. Just – I think.

LOUIE: We can't live here for ever with you thinking I'm a ghost.

ROBERT: Come on God. Sock it to me. Guilt! Come on!

(Tries out a rather dry scream.)

LOUIE: Be quiet.

ROBERT (scream): I'm guilty. (Scream.) I'm haunted. That's it. (Scream.)

(He goes off, emitting these dry and unlovely noises.)

BOBBIE: Louie?

KATE: Jim?

LOUIE: It's an *idee fixe.* I'm stuck.

(Scream off.)

Oh shut up!

KATE (calling): Who said that?

LOUIE: Louie.

KATE: Aren't you dead?

BOBBIE: No he's not.

ROBERT (off): He is, he is!

(Scream. ADA enters to LOUIE.)

ADA: Who's doing it?

LOUIE: Robert.

ADA: I thought you were Jim.

LOUIE: You said I was Kate.

ADA: You *are* Louie, aren't you.

LOUIE: Yes.

ADA: Who's he shot then?

   (Dry scream.)

   Oh lord.

   (She goes. Another scream.)

LOUIE: You missed, you silly bastard. I'm alive.

   (He lies down. Enter ROBERT to KATE.)

KATE (clutches her rug to her): No!

ROBERT: No what?

KATE: You mustn't kill me.

ROBERT: That's it. Go at me.

KATE: Go at you?

ROBERT: Tell me I'm vile. Tell me I'm wicked.

KATE: You haven't killed Jim.

ROBERT: That's it. Think the worst of me. Murderer. The sort of person nubile girls are frightened of. Well done. (Screams.) Come on guilt.

   (Goes off emitting screams.)

KATE (calling): Jim?

   (Enter ADA to BOBBIE.)

ADA: Where is he?

BOBBIE: Who?

ADA: You're all so unhelpful. I have to reach him before he goes mad.

   (She goes off.)

BOBBIE: He's just mistaken, Ada. Louie? Louie!

   (Enter JIM crawling towards LOUIE.)

LOUIE (replying to BOBBIE): Stay where you are!

   (JIM falls on his stomach. He looks round nervously.
   Two or three screams.)

JIM: All right now?

LOUIE (seeing him): What are you doing?

JIM: Keeping out of sight.

LOUIE: Someone'll trip over you there.

JIM: Can I hide under your bed?

LOUIE: Certainly.

> (JIM makes for it. ROBERT enters to BOBBIE, speaking as he enters.)

ROBERT: All I wanted was the sky to be blue again, the birds to sing, the grass to grow in short springy turves. Was that so wrong?

BOBBIE: No.

ROBERT: And yet there is his blood boltered corpse haunting the desert vastness. Guilt, you see.

BOBBIE: No, Robert.

ROBERT: I can't seem to get it flowing properly.

BOBBIE: Look Robert, let's face things squarely. Louie is not dead.

ROBERT: I've just seen his ghost.

BOBBIE (getting short): Are you or are you not going to be honest.

ROBERT: Not if it means saying what you're saying, no.

> (He goes off, muttering 'I am guilty'.)

BOBBIE (following with her rug): You are not.

ROBERT (off): I am.

BOBBIE (off): You're not.

ROBERT (off): I'll bloody shoot you if you don't shut up.

BOBBIE (off): Now Robert, let's view this sensibly.

ROBERT (off): That's what I am doing.

> (Enter ADA to KATE.)

ADA: Find Jim, and collect Bobbie if you see her, avoiding Robert, and get to my place where you'll find Louie. I'll have a last attempt at raising Moles. All right?

KATE: Can't I come with you?

ADA: You must get the others.

KATE: I think I'm getting tummy ache.

ADA: I hope you aren't pregnant already.

> (They are off, KATE with rug, etc. Enter to LOUIE, ROBERT and BOBBIE.)

BOBBIE: You merely *think* you've shot him because that's what you think you've wanted to do all your life. Really though, what you've been wanting deep inside you, in the deepest levels of your being, as far down as it's possible to explore, is to love him. Isn't that so?

ROBERT (eyeing LOUIE): No.

BOBBIE: If you can admit that, your guilt will evaporate.

ROBERT: I have no guilt. That's the trouble. I admit to you, the ghost of my unhappy victim, that I have no guilt for having shot you. No guilt, and no pleasure. I can't feel anything.

BOBBIE: Well bloody hell, have we spent all this time feeling sorry for you, trying to help you, offering you heaven knows what, just to find the whole thing has been a try-on and you're perfectly balanced? For God's sake just pull yourself together.

(ROBERT swings his rifle back to hit her. ADA and KATE enter.)

ADA: Halt!

(He stops.)

You must learn to obey other kinds of command besides that one.

ROBERT: She said I was balanced.

ADA: She's a very silly girl. Kate, take them all away and try not to see the spectacle Moles is making of himself. We'll come along at breakfast time if we're ready. Off you go. You can walk now, Jim.

(ROBERT and ADA are left alone.)

ROBERT: I am *not* balanced.

ADA (sitting on the bed): Of course not.

ROBERT: I just can't feel anything.

ADA: Have you shot him?

ROBERT: That's my business.

ADA (sings): If I were married
I would love you as a son.
You would live and be well,
And I would be one.

We would think about life
And life would spring,
The year would flow
Like a rich green thing.

But I am not married,
I am not a mother,
I'm man and woman both,
And I have no children,
And I'm a sore half-thing.

(The songs seems to end as if it isn't finished.)

ROBERT: I hate the songs you sing.

(The lights change to dawn.)

ADA: It's breakfast time.

ROBERT: I don't want any breakfast.

(ADA gets up and packs up her bed. ROBERT sees something off-stage which holds his attention.)

ADA: Something warm inside you always makes a difference.

ROBERT: Look at that Paula. She's enjoying it.

ADA (also watching): You must remember she has a body as well as a uniform. They both need exercising.

ROBERT (feels his stomach): There's my ulcer. It's the first time in ten years.

ADA: Warm milk. Come alone.

(She takes his hand.)

ROBERT: Either you infiltrate, or you enjoy it. (Shouts.) Bitch! bloody female bitch!

(They go off. Enter MOLES, wearing his hat and an enormous purple bath robe.)

MOLES (to audience): What a sheik among men I am! One always knew, but one allowed one's ego to die under the weight of one's philosophy, one's devotion to the modest way. It's so hard to love one's neighbour as oneself when oneself is so remarkable. I did it. I led my flock as modestly as any bishop, but we are what we are, and if we are superb, what can we do about it? One must beware of fantasizing, I suppose. I'm tempted to tell you what she said. 'You're too good for me,' she said. Now is that a fact or isn't it? If it is a fact, what do I do about it? I condescend. I lower myself generously to her love. On occasions. If it isn't a fact, and it may after all not be a fact, why did she say it? Because she is deluded! She is in love with me!

ADA (off): Breakfast!

MOLES: I don't feel like eating. I wonder if I've gone beyond the material world altogether and become pure mind? Pure spiritual Moles? Molissimus, Most High Moles?

ADA (off): Breakfast!

MOLES (to audience): Most released and ineffable of creatures.

(PAULA comes in unseen, tunic only, carrying trousers. She watches as she does up some buttons.)

MOLES: I am what I am and what I am cannot be hid. She felt my presence. She made me see.

PAULA: All those years with the soldiers, their awful jokes — the barrack room lady, the officer giving and getting a thrill.

MOLES (pitying): Aaaah.

PAULA: Am I in love with you, really?

MOLES: Yes of course.

PAULA: I'm not unworthy?

MOLES: No. No, not at all. No, no of course you aren't.

PAULA: One day, when you've taught me everything there is to know, perhaps I too can have a hat like that.

(While MOLES speaks PAULA beckons off-stage and JIM comes on. She whispers to him. Amazed, he lies flat on the floor. So does she. They are prostrating themselves.)

MOLES: It does rather suit me, doesn't it. I never used to fancy the Roman church, because it seemed to have its roots deep in materialism. Now I'm not so sure.

(He sees the prostrate bodies.)

It is just possible that I'm being made a fool of, but I don't think so.

(To the two of them.)

Please get up.

(PAULA begins to do the Arab wailing.)

Very good. Very good indeed. Do get up.

(They both do the wailing.)

Stop!

(They both do.)

Arise.

(They both do, but keep their heads down on PAULA's lead.)

You make me feel very uncomfortable. I think I'll just go and have a last bath.

(He speaks low to PAULA.)

You are serious, aren't you?

(She goes down on one knee.)

Yes, all right.

(He goes out. PAULA stands up.)

PAULA: Parade! Attention!

(JIM snaps into position.)

We have successfully adapted to a new situation for the first time in our lives. The oasis is ours.

JIM: Whose?

PAULA: Mine. Where's Robert?

JIM: He thinks he's shot Louie Thompson.

PAULA: Has he?

JIM: I'm afraid not.

PAULA: Mess. I turn my back for half a minute and the place becomes a pigsty. You can't be trusted, can you. Robert! Fall in! Robert!

(Enter ADA and ROBERT, ROBERT with a cup of tea and a piece of toast, and marmalade. PAULA pulls on trousers.)

I've no idea what happened last night but it won't happen again, is that clear? This oasis is ours and I got it and I didn't get any help from either of you. Down by the pool you will find a sedan chair and by now you will find in it the man you will learn to love and honour as the wisest man in the world. Please carry him here ready to address the assembled company. Parade attention. About turn. By the front quick march. Left right, left right, left right.

(JIM leaves. ROBERT munches. She sees him.)

Robert?

(ROBERT approaches PAULA. He spits a mixture of toast and milk all over her.)

I'll deal with that later.

ROBERT: Now.

PAULA: Order is order, Robert. Go and get the sedan chair.

ROBERT: You enjoyed it all last night, didn't you? I shan't forget that.

(He goes saying to ADA:)

It was me shot Louie Thompson, all by myself, while she was enjoying herself.

PAULA: Captain Ada, please.

ADA: Here, let me.

(She advances with a hanky and begins to wipe PAULA.)

PAULA: I think you ought to realize — for goodness sake.

ADA: Milk goes sour very quickly in this heat, and you'll smell horrid.

PAULA: Thank you. (Rubs at her clothes herself.) I think you ought to realize that there isn't room for all of us here.

ADA: No?

PAULA: And I'm in a pretty commanding position, Captain.

ADA: It didn't look to me as if you could go on doing that much longer.

PAULA: I have great will power, and can do anything if I make up my mind to it.

ADA (calmly): No amount of will power on your part can make him want you once you've lost your careless abandon. You'll grow old, and you'll pretend and it'll show. You chest will flatten to yellow scrags, and your greying hair will thin out in the sun. The veins in your body will wrinkle like ropey string where everything was once velvet, and they'll be fishy blue and probably painful. You'll get piles, fallen arches, sun blindness, deafness, tooth ache — those teeth will yellow up like horses — and all this will stop a virile man like Moles wanting to make love to you, not just because you're ugly but because an element of duty will have entered into your love making. Especially will it happen if you make him think you really care for him, because he'll remember how it was before he realized he'd been blinded, by your now faded physique. And if Bobbie and Kate are still here to remind him of what it was like when you started your position will become desperate, dry and remote. What it won't be is commanding. Moles will turn to me, eventually, not for love, but to help him run the oasis. To me who has plenty of time to read before going to bed at night, and therefore time to develop a lively mind.

PAULA: I can have you removed.

ADA: I don't think so. There's breakfast if you want it.

(She turns to go. There is a shot off-stage.)

What's he shot this time?

PAULA: It's what he shoots next time that may prove interesting.

(Enter BOBBIE and KATE.)

KATE: Ada. He's shot himself.

ADA: Who has?

BOBBIE (to ADA): What did you do that drove him to it?

ADA: You mean Robert?

BOBBIE: He'd have snapped out of it if you hadn't mothered him.

KATE: They're bringing him in.

(PAULA snaps to attention and begins to hum the last post, her hand at the salute. MOLES and JIM carry an improvised sedan chair with ROBERT sitting bolt upright, blood coming from his forehead. MOLES is not wearing his hat. Everyone looks at PAULA who fades out and lowers her hand.)

LOUIE: He spoke to me, the ghost. He said we were all beneath contempt and he'd meet me in the life hereafter.

BOBBIE (to corpse): You silly thing, Robert you silly *thing.*

ADA: I *tried* to love him. I didn't exactly succeed but I was a good listener.

LOUIE: We could spend some time putting together the story of the cowslip in the thermos flask.

PAULA: The what?

LOUIE: Well, it seems that one day, at the Goring Gap, a particularly favourite place for picnics in Robert's family —

MOLES: One moment. We have all been arrogant in the extreme, a thing which I at least came here to avoid. If we hadn't been arrogant, this man might've lived. Let's go and bury him and remember that.

(They take the sedan chair out. All except PAULA follow.)

PAULA (to the audience): I've lost. We'll say I've learnt my lesson and I don't mind losing in the least. People always do say that.

(She smiles and walks off after the others.)

END

MUSIC for THE LAND OF PALMS by DAVID CREGAN

MUSIC by MARTIN DUNCAN & BRIAN PROTHEROE

Steel in the Legion

There's No Peace

Oh my name is Moles

Love or duty

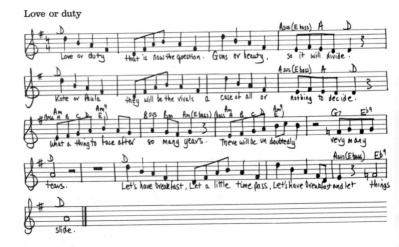

Who'll be the winner?

I have a hat

I have a hat, a beautiful hat, a mystical hat that is holy at that.

Oh what a hat —

I want to live

Add 1+3 I want to live, I don't want to die. There's not much but I've for
2. You want to live, and I want a man. I want to have him as

3. You want to live. I want a Man. I want to

1+3. me in the sky. Save me from death at the hands of a man-i-ac,
2. Soon as I can. Are these two problems re-mote ly conn-ected,

3. have him as soon as I can. Are these two problems conn-ected,

Dm. (last time D)

1+3. I want to live and I tear I shall die.
2. You wanting li- ife, and me wanting man?

3. You wanting life, and me wanting man?

If I were married

if I were married I would love you as a son. You would live and be well, and I would be one. We would think about life and life would spring, the year would flow like a rich green thing. But I am not married, I am not a mother, I'm man and woman both, and I have no children, And I'm a sore half-thing.

Liebestraum

LIEBESTRAUM was first presented by the Midlands Arts Centre Repertory Company at the Studio Theatre, Birmingham, on 11 December 1970 with the following cast:

JANE	*Lesley Joseph*
SYLVIA	*Jane Briers*
PAUL	*Neil McLauchlan*
ROBERT	*Derek Fuke*

Directed by Philip Hedley

The scene is a room with a table and two chairs. There is an exit to upstairs which has three steps. It is important that the three footsteps people make going up and down these steps can clearly be heard. There is another entrance, from outside, but I don't think a door is necessary. The table should have a shelf from which mugs of cocoa can be instantly produced and also breakfast. Breakfast is just one plate of food and a knife and fork. The table should end up covered in mugs of cocoa. JANE is standing in a mackintosh gazing at a cup of cocoa, hands in pockets. Note: The scene is the same for both houses.

JANE (to audience): Ours is a modern marriage. You need four in a modern marriage and at the moment there's only three in ours. So there's the symbol of my sex life, cocoa every other night.

ROBERT (off upstairs): Is that Jane?

JANE: Yes. Have you —

ROBERT: Yes.

(Steps coming down stairs. JANE covers her eyes with one hand. Enter SYLVIA doing up mac.)

SYLVIA: It's a pity you don't like my Paul as much as I like your Robert. Someone always has to get up and go home. (Seeing JANE with hand over eyes.) Whatever is it?

JANE: I can't face you.

SYLVIA (sitting down): Aaah. Let's have a little talk. Now. What is a man?

JANE: Mine is the man I love.

SYLVIA: Is that enough, Jane.

JANE: The western family unit is acknowledged to be too small —

SYLVIA: Too inward —

JANE: Too repressive. I know.

SYLVIA: So we're very lucky with our little foursome and we should cherish it.

JANE (hands off eyes): But it's not a foursome, it's a threesome.

SYLVIA: It's what I call Mother Nature's way. (She picks up cocoa and starts to drink it.)

JANE (sees SYLVIA with drink): Put down my cocoa, Sylvia.

SYLVIA (doing so): It's cold.

JANE: It's mine.

SYLVIA (going off outside): There you are, you see. Possessive.

(JANE gazes at cocoa and pushes it away.)

JANE (to audience): Another symbol of my sex life. He gets it ready for me every other night and I fiddle about till it's gone cold. But I do try to please.

(She goes upstairs slowly. Enter SYLVIA from outside. She doesn't take her mac off during the scene.)

SYLVIA (calling): Paul! (no reply — jauntily.) Pau - aul! (No reply — sharply.) Paul! (No reply — to the audience.) I'm not worried. He understands how insecure I used to be and how the perfect balance has to be struck, like diabetics.

(SYLVIA takes out a cup of cocoa.)

If he finds his own other partner, of course, we could end up in a complicated geometrical pattern. I doubt if that would give quite the security we have just now.

(Enter PAUL, also wearing mac, open.)

PAUL: Sylvia!

SYLVIA: Paul!

PAUL: Well, well, well!

SYLVIA: I see. Cocoa. (She puts another mug on the table.)

PAUL: I realize from your voice the fact that you realize from my voice the fact that I've tagged onto a conga line of my own discovery. I think you think that I've acted stupidly and I think you've been thinking that you *would* think that ever since you thought that what you thought would happen *would* happen.

SYLVIA: Yes.

PAULA: You've also decided what you're going to tell the doctor tomorrow, that young general practitioner who also studied philosophy, English Literature, anthropology and psychology, and therefore feels himself qualified to set us up like a domestic water system, male and female ends in one big circle, all cemented in, happily finding novelty within the limits of civilized society.

SYLVIA: I'm going to tell him you've buggered it up.

PAUL: I knew it.

SYLVIA: You're very what we call aggressive tonight, Paul. Sit down.

PAUL: Yes. (Sits. To audience.) I'm not usually aggressive. Note that.

SYLVIA: I expect you're feeling guilty.

PAUL (considering): That would mean I thought I'd done something bad.

SYLVIA: Anti-social, as we say.

PAUL: No, I don't feel guilty.

SYLVIA: You *have* done something inconvenient.

PAUL: Possibly.

SYLVIA: And you feel confused.

PAUL: Yes. Right. (To audience.) Confused. And also what with running for the bus and everything, tired.

SYLVIA: The question is, Paul, was it worth it?

PAUL: At the time.

SYLVIA: I wonder if living for the moment is enough.

PAUL: I wonder that, too. But when *do* you decide if something's worth it, if not at the moment it happens? Afterwards? When you're old? When you're dead? It's quite a question actually.

SYLVIA: It's *the* question.

PAUL: For instance, would I do it again?

SYLVIA: Probably.

PAUL: It was worth it, then.

SYLVIA: Can you tell me, Paul, from your heart of hearts, exactly *what* it was worth?

PAUL: Imponderables. There they stretch away in front of me, imponderable upon imponderable. Suppose it makes you unhappy? That'll make Robert unhappy. That'll make Jane unhappy. I'd hate that to happen so that'd make me unhappy.

SYLVIA: Quite.

PAUL: Supposing there are children?

SYLVIA: You haven't been *that* inconvenient, surely.

PAUL: It *is* a thought, and I am a thinking man in my way.

SYLVIA: We'd better take our cocoa up to bed, Paul, and think a bit further.

(She goes upstairs with her cup of cocoa.)

PAUL (to audience): Values. Puzzling things. Try to avoid them myself, but they keep coming up.

(He goes upstairs with his cocoa. Enter ROBERT from upstairs, hat in hand.)

ROBERT: Hullo. Where's breakfast?

(JANE comes downstairs, pulling down her sweater and bringing mac.)

ROBERT (sitting at table): Is our marriage creaking a little?

(JANE plonks down breakfast in front of him.)

I think you should answer me.

JANE: If I say yes, you'll say 'It's out at last', and if I say no, you'll say 'You're blinding yourself to reality'.

ROBERT (eating): There's a loss of spontaneity about our routine, Jane, which doesn't satisfy me like I used to be satisfied. We used to bound from thing to thing like merry squirrels, and now we don't. It's beginning to affect my work, and I find my in-tray isn't keeping pace with my out-tray any more.

JANE: I love you Robert.

ROBERT: Love is quite splendid and quite splendidly we manage it, throwing it into relief in various contemporary ways. Only recently, someone said of me, 'There goes a truly three-dimensional man.' But it takes patience and energy to manage a three-dimensional life, and, if I may point the moral, sympathy from each dimension it is lived in. You are one of my dimensions.

JANE: I didn't sleep last night. I love you.

ROBERT: Love can't be allowed to ruin our marriage, Jane. What's wrong with Paul?

JANE: I just don't want to.

ROBERT: We all have to do things we don't want.

JANE: I was brought up to believe –

ROBERT: Then you were brought up wrong.

SYLVIA (off outside): Hullo!

ROBERT (shouting to her): Not now, I've got a train to catch.

(Enter SYLVIA in her mac still.)

SYLVIA: I'm glad I'm in time. I don't know what to do. I don't know – I don't know what – Oh dear.

(She sits down gazing rather blankly ahead.)

ROBERT (to JANE): She's had a shock.

SYLVIA: Paul's joined another circuit.

ROBERT (at JANE): What? This is what comes of your unbridled fidelity! (More generally.) We'll find ourselves part of a larger community before we know where we are, with all the loss of sovereignty that will entail.

(Pause.)

JANE: Would anyone like cocoa?

SYLVIA: I have to say this.

ROBERT (finishing for her): My wife hasn't pulled her weight. Selfishness.

SYLVIA: Hedonism.

ROBERT (despairing shrug): The welfare state attitude to pleasure.

JANE (to audience): I can see what's going to happen. I'll be left by myself, running a babysitting service on alternate evenings. A sex widow. I'll be burdened for ever with the knowledge that I'm out of phase, my pace-maker having got a rhythm of its own, susceptible only to that one mistaken law with which I've grown up, the primacy of warm relationships.

ROBERT and SYLVIA: Exactly.

ROBERT: We did all read that book before we started.

SYLVIA: With original Scandinavian woodcuts. Let's have a little talk.

ROBERT (glancing at watch): The 8.30 is pulling out.

SYLVIA: I left my Paul at home, all on his own. He's not on mornings now, so go and talk to him. Explain the poverty of spirit that comes with coldness. Tell him of the ashes to be found in sex without warmth. Tell him that while you offer him the jam of a warm relationship, I give him the bread and butter of security. Which he gives back to me while I get jam from Robert. Tell him that, Jane, in simple terms, because he isn't very quick, though willing and then get into bed with him and show him.

JANE: No.

SYLVIA: Why ever not? He's terribly strong when he wants to be.

ROBERT: Oh! I've had a ghastly insight. Sylvia, I've got to raise a delicate matter.

SYLVIA: We're all friends here, I hope.

ROBERT: Class.

SYLVIA (thumping the table and standing): I'm just as bourgeois as the next woman, and if I'm not, I'm proud of my origins!

ROBERT: Is it snobbery, Jane, that stops you having a warm relationship with Paul, a skilled labourer?

JANE: I just don't want to do it with him.

ROBERT: If we all lived in a middle class housing association there'd be no problem.

SYLVIA: If I'm good enough for Robert, Paul's good enough for you. I'm going to have a turn, I know. I'll have to see the doctor.

JANE: Before I married you I lived for ages with a porter at Covent Garden.

SYLVIA: Now that *is* different. There's skilled and there's unskilled, always has been.

ROBERT: And Covent Garden porters are often intellectuals.

JANE: He was jolly, and he said I was the snuggest bit of fur he'd ever put a nail through.

(ROBERT and SYLVIA both freeze up.)

ROBERT (silently): Well! (Aloud!) The 8.35's gone, the 8.40's going, so it looks like the 8.47. Shall I walk you to the doctor's, Mrs Smith?

SYLVIA: Thank you Mr Brown. That's very civil of you.

ROBERT (as they leave for outside): And we're out before she's used a four-letter word.

(They disappear.)

JANE (shouting after them): There's no four-letter words in all this! I haven't had a good four-letter word since everything became so regular. It's more like syrup of figs than sex. (To audience.) Perhaps that's the answer. If I went at Paul like a nymphomaniac, and played the D. H. Lawrence bit as hard as possible, perhaps I could resolve it somehow. I'm not wild about it but (Picking up mac.) I can't go on in limbo. (Going off outside.) And I needn't go on if I don't like it.

(SYLVIA in a spotlight. The DOCTOR's voice can either be spoken by SYLVIA herself, as if it is all a fantasy, or can be spoken off-stage.)

SYLVIA: It's this way, Doctor, it's my double nature, my schizophrenia, my late-night Hollywood movie syndrome coming up again. I know it's all in my mind, but it's in my body where I feel it.

DOCTOR: You need more, Sylvia?

SYLVIA: No, I don't need more. I haven't a lot of time for more. But I need – how shall I put it?

DOCTOR: Better quality?

SYLVIA: No, no, it's all high fidelity stuff. I want to be sure it'll go on, that's all. I have told you, haven't I, that my uncle raped me at eleven, that I was the breadwinner by twelve, raising six brothers and sisters, all older, none of whom paid the least attention to me, and that because I hadn't time to do my home work I became withdrawn? I have told you, haven't I, Doctor?

DOCTOR: You've told me, Sylvia, and I've reassured you that your trouble lies precisely there. You can always take comfort from your upbringing if you find yourself at odds with society.

SYLVIA: Thank you, Doctor. And I can tell them that they must settle down properly, or I'll go mad?

DOCTOR: Yes.

SYLVIA: Dear Doctor. (To audience.) I can't honestly tell you how much of that's true, but I can tell you this. It frightens the men like hell if I pull it strong enough.

(She exits from the spotlight. The spotlight goes out. Enter JANE, wearing a mac. She stands defiantly by the table.)

JANE (calling): I've come!

(PAUL enters from upstairs.)

PAUL: I think you ought to know –

JANE: I bring you sun and rock and peaty smelling earth. I'm full of rhythms and fires and smoking clouds of spring rain forcing buds into quivering flowers of damp and joyful everything. (She swings her mac open. She is wearing panties and bra.) Awaken me. I sleep, in comparative virginity.

PAUL (to audience): Values again. (To JANE.) I think you ought to know –

JANE: I do know. Awaken me and don't waste time.

PAUL: I can't, you're wearing underclothes.

JANE: Then take them off!

PAUL: You take them off!

JANE: I can't!

PAUL: Why not?

JANE: I'm shy.

PAUL: We don't know one another well enough for this, do we?

JANE: If we don't know one another well enough for this, we don't know one another well enough for that, I suppose.

PAUL: Cocoa? (Takes a cup.)

JANE: You think I'm inhibited. You don't mind feeling sorry for me in passing, but it's rather a long haul to know me well enough to go to bed with. It's instant orgasms for you, isn't it. You and my husband and your wife. I don't know why you don't sit round in one cosy circle, knee to knee and –

PAUL: Jane!

JANE: You could even drink your cocoa, once your free hand adjusted to the rhythm. A regular feast of warm milk and sugar, satisfying every mediocre appetite that floated up.

PAUL: What dreadful things to say!

JANE: You haven't *kissed* a girl in years.

PAUL (surprised): No.

JANE: You haven't thought of anything above the navel since you hit on Sylvia.

PAUL: You take me back to my adolescence. May I kiss you?

JANE: Certainly.

(They kiss. Enter from outside SYLVIA, wearing mac.)

SYLVIA: Oh well done! (She gets the cocoa.) Only not on the ground floor for heavens sake. Curtains open, broad daylight, no attempt at hole in the corner, what are you thinking of?

(She drinks her cocoa. Then –)

Don't fiddle around kissing. Go to bed right away and get it out of your systems.

(They part.)

JANE: How surprising, I'm in love with you.

PAUL: I'm in love with you.

SYLVIA: Aah. (To audience.) Aren't they sweet? (To the couple.) Off you go then. (As they go upstairs, to the audience.) Things are working out after all. (Drinks cocoa, suddenly shocked.) My God, it's the wrong day. (To upstairs.)

You filthy pair of adulterers, you're messing up the time-table! He's mine till tomorrow breakfast!

JANE (off): Sorry!

SYLVIA: What d'you mean, sorry?

JANE (off): I mean (Silence. Then —) Ah!

SYLVIA (shocked): This is going to bring on my paranoia. (To upstairs.) Nobody loves me I'm a failure where's the arsenic? (Silence. Angrily.) Arsenic! (Silence.) Arsenic, I said where's the bloody arsenic!

PAUL (off): I'll be down soon, love.

SYLVIA: Oh will you! You needn't think I'm going to wait here to be brutalised by the silence of a man who doesn't notice when I need him. You needn't think I'm going to let myself be twisted by the cultural stress involved in knowing he'll fail to go on the afternoon shift and leave us too short of cash to reach the standard of living my intelligence requires! (Silence.) I hope you're not listening because if you are you're being very cruel. (Silence.) (To audience.) And Robert's at work and I don't feel like cocoa — as a matter of fact, I *am* a bit upset.

(She goes off outside. Enter ROBERT.)

ROBERT: Home, darling . . . (Silence. To audience.) Creaking, you see. (Removes hat, gets cocoa.) Creak, creak creak. Life has to run smoothly or not at all. If it doesn't run smoothly you can't cope with pressure, and pressure is the *sine qua non* of modern life. If it weren't for pressure, gracious living would elude us completely. (He drinks.) In five years, I hope to be a man who makes at least one first-class airflight a week with a very thin brief-case and immaculate trousers. I am currently a socialist, because up to, though not including, directorship level it is a required attitude.

(Enter SYLVIA, rather sad.)

SYLVIA: Robert?

ROBERT: It's the wrong night.

SYLVIA: Paul has missed the afternoon shift altogether.

ROBERT: You mean they've done it?

SYLVIA: They're still doing it. It's gone all wrong, like cancer.

ROBERT (to audience): Crisis. This is where the men stand out from the boys. (To SYLVIA.) Cocoa, Sylvia?

SYLVIA: I couldn't.

ROBERT: Oh. (Slight pause.) What do you think of Poulenc as a composer?

SYLVIA: What?

ROBERT: We have to talk about something, and I can't bear to be banal.

SYLVIA: It's what we're going to do we have to talk about.

ROBERT: I think I'll go to bed with a book.

SYLVIA: Can't I come?

ROBERT (severely): It's the wrong night! We mustn't *all* lose our heads. I think you'll find, by and large, when the reckoning is made, at the end of the day everything will find its own level. More or less.

(He goes upstairs to bed.)

SYLVIA (to audience): Everyone in bed but me. I don't think it's ever happened before.

(She goes off too outside.)

JANE (off): I think I ought to go.

PAUL (off): Why?

JANE (off): There *are* others.

PAUL (off): Where?

JANE (off): Try showing some of this to your girl on the circuit.

PAUL (off): Oh! You show Robert.

JANE (off): Of course.

(They come down the steps hand in hand, wearing macs.)

JANE (to audience): At the moment we're very happy.

PAUL (to audience): And if we're lucky it might go on.

JANE (to audience): In the meantime, we're going to let our light so shine before men that they see our good work and glorify whatever is responsible for it.

(They go off together. SYLVIA enters in spotlight.)

SYLVIA: Things aren't what they were all of a sudden, Doctor. I wonder if you could give me more practical help, if you know what I mean.

DOCTOR: The Hypocratic Oath prevents me.

SYLVIA: I'll go private if it helps.

DOCTOR: An oath is an oath, Sylvia.

SYLVIA: I knew you'd say that. So brave. There it lies between us, then, an unrequited mirage, the Great What Might Have Been. I find that comforting.

DOCTOR: Dear Sylvia.

SYLVIA: Dear John. I can last a little longer now it's out.

(She leaves. The spotlight goes out. Enter PAUL from outside, mac over his arm.)

PAUL (to audience): Wrong night. She was playing racing demon with her husband. Sylvia!

(He goes off upstairs. Enter from stairs ROBERT in pyjamas and slippers.)

ROBERT (very disturbed): Jane! I'm surprised at you.

JANE (off upstairs): Why?

ROBERT: You've never done that before, and I hope you'll never do it again. It was carnal. I'm going to Sylvia to have my balance restored.

(He snatches up mac and goes off.)

JANE (off upstairs): I was only loving you.

(Enter from outside SYLVIA.)

SYLVIA: Robert! Robert I have to speak to you. Wrong night or not, you must pretend to be the Doctor.

(She goes off upstairs. Enter from outside ROBERT wearing mac.)

ROBERT: Sylvia! If Paul's in bed with you, throw him out. (He goes upstairs saying –) I've had a very nasty experience.

PAUL (off upstairs): There's no help here, I'm afraid.

(ROBERT comes down the stairs.)

ROBERT: Good heavens, where's she got to? I always said we should have diaries and then this sort sort of muddle wouldn't happen.

(PAUL comes down the stairs in pyjamas.)

PAUL: She's probably fantasizing with the Doctor.

ROBERT: Fantasizing? You mean her uncle didn't rape her?

PAUL: I'd like you to know that I think your wife is beautiful.

ROBERT: He must've done. It's half her attraction that she's never got over it.

PAUL: I love her, and as far as one can judge these things, I'm likely to go on. If you divorce her, I'd like you to give me first refusal.

ROBERT: *Something* must've happened. People are always interfered with in the working classes, that's their thing. With us, you know, it's more Byronic. I was passionately adored by every member of the first fifteen, and just as I was settling to a really good season, the captain's favourite in the showers, worshipping every muscle in his body, I found to my amazement I'd been seduced by the lady catering manager. Try facing that with a stiff upper lip, which is all you're allowed at a public school.

PAUL: If that's settled, then I'll say good evening.

(Enter SYLVIA with her hand on her brow, wearing her mac.)

SYLVIA: There was a woman in my bed! I shall never be the same!

PAUL (glancing upstairs): *Your* bed?

ROBERT (to PAUL): *My* bed, I should think.

SYLVIA: Good heavens! I've never seen either of you in pyjamas before.

PAUL: What happened?

SYLVIA: She kissed me thinking I was you and then apologized for not being a man. It was Jane.

ROBERT: She should apologize to me for not being a lady.

SYLIVA: I don't mind which of you it is, but one of you please come up and pretend to be the doctor. (She goes off upstiars.)

PAUL: I don't think I could do that.

ROBERT: Is it a game of some sort?

(Enter JANE from outside in her nightie, mac over shoulders like a cape.)

JANE (flinging off mac): Robert!

PAUL: Jane!

ROBERT (pulling his mac tighter): No.

JANE (going for him): I want to make you happy.

ROBERT: I have to be compassionate with Sylvia.

(ROBERT rushes upstairs.)

JANE: You've been quick.

PAUL: Wrong night.

JANE: Then get up there with Sylvia and send Robert down to me at once. (He doesn't move.) We have to show them.

PAUL: It's getting less imperative.

JANE: It mustn't.

(He goes. She speaks to the audience.)

Fortunately there are no children, so there won't be any broken homes if what's going to happen really happens.

(ROBERT comes from downstairs backwards, having been pushed. Still in mac and pyjamas.)

ROBERT (to upstairs): I'd really rather —

JANE: Darling!

ROBERT: NO! I refuse! (He backs away.) There'll be nothing left of me to deal with pressure if you go on like you did just now. Where will gracious living go and what about my first-class airflight and my socialism? Cocoa!

(He grabs two mugs and fends her off with them.)

JANE: It comes to this. What do you really want from life?

(Enter SYLVIA, mac on but undone.)

SYLVIA: The Doctor.

(Enter PAUL from upstairs, pyjama jacket gone.)

PAUL: I'm offering to tear myself apart and give a bit of it to you.

SYLVIA (getting it): Cocoa.

ROBERT (referring to JANE): For God's sake keep her down here.

(Dashes upstairs still holding the cocoa.)

JANE: I only want to help you, Robert!

(She leaps after him. There is a cry and a crash.)

SYLVIA: He's broken the cocoa mugs.

PAUL: *She's* broken the cocoa mugs.

(PAUL leaps at her. She dodges him and screams. Enter ROBERT pulling his mac about him. JANE follows in pursuit. Together ROBERT and SYLVIA shout 'No! No! No!' until there is a pause. Together, JANE and PAUL say the following speech, pursuing the others round the stage.)

PAUL and JANE: I love you Robert/Sylvia, and I've always loved you, and we can't expect it to be regulated or do it while we look the other way.

ROBERT (turning with SYLVIA to face them again, grabbing cocoa mugs, speaking to JANE): I warn you! I may well think about divorce if you insist on raping me.

SYLVIA (to PAUL): And me! I've never been submitted to such foulness outside my imagination.

PAUL (turning to JANE): In that case —

JANE: We have tried —

(They kiss.)

ROBERT (pontificating to audience): We aren't in this world for fun. It's our duty to find reasons for our pleasures, and explain to the world that we only do certain things because we can't help it, and not because we like them. Recreation is not fun, but re-creation, as any puritan will tell you —

SYLVIA: Look!

ROBERT (seeing the kiss): Emotionalism! This is your fault, carelessly exposing the innermost parts of your soul.

ROBERT (begins his speech): In five years, I hope to be a man who makes at least one first-class airflight.

SYLVIA (simultaneously begins her speech): I have told you haven't I, that my uncle raped me at eleven.

(The other two go upstairs. 'Liebestraum' plays.)

END

George Reborn

GEORGE REBORN was first presented on the B.B.C. programme 'Full House' on 20 January 1973 with the following cast:

GEORGE, a rather indeterminate young man	*Ronald Pickup*
ANNA, a well-defined young woman, possibly with sweeping hair	*Angela Downe*
CHARLEY, an older man, greying, wearing a white shirt, a square, dark trousers, and a cardigan	*Tenniel Evans*
AMY, a kindly shop girl	*Stephanie Turner*
ALICE, a stringy shop girl	*Paula Wilcox*
ERM, an earthy girl	*Sharon Duce*
SIDNEY, a young man with glasses	*Tim Wylton*
ORCHESTRA	*The Gabrieli Wind Ensemble*

It was subsequently presented by the Richmond Fringe Theatre Group at the Orange Tree, Richmond, on 2 February 1973 with the following cast:

GEORGE	*Geoffrey Beevers*
ANNA	*Patricia Garwood*
CHARLEY	*Vernon Joyner*
AMY	*Caroline John*
ALICE	*Sheilah Felvin*
SIDNEY	*Bernard Holley*
ERM	*Isobel Nisbet*
TAPE RECORDER	*Jill Posener*

Both productions were directed by Sam Walters.

Enter GEORGE, a rather indeterminate young man, and ANNA, a well-defined and well-dressed young woman who sits down on the stage. GEORGE begins to conduct the Orchestra. They play some suitable atmospheric music, perhaps 'L'Apres-midi d'un faune', while he speaks, and continues to conduct.

GEORGE (to audience): Anna and I often come here on summer evenings, to this rocky stream surrounded by these pines. It stays warm here very late, and smells of peat. We don't often make love, however, because Anna doesn't like me very much. C'est la vie.

(He stops the Orchestra.)

Thank you.

ANNA: Are you still on fire, George?

GEORGE: Yes.

ANNA: Oh lord.

GEORGE: Yes.

ANNA: When you're deeply moved you crumple up, don't you?

GEORGE: I don't.

ANNA: You go like a baked apple.

(She laughs to herself.)

GEORGE: I don't think you understand me.

ANNA (laughing gently to herself): Oh yes I do.

GEORGE: Can't you see me as a hero, doing surprising things in a deerskin?

ANNA (lying down): Good heavens no.

GEORGE: I have horrid and revolting thoughts, you know.

ANNA: Oh George.

GEORGE: Revolting thoughts of great nobility.

ANNA: Do lie down and be quiet.

GEORGE: Quiet? With all this raging storm inside me?

ANNA: It's such a pleasant evening.

GEORGE: I'll try.

(He lies down beside her. Enter CHARLEY, an older man, elegantly dressed. He immediately conducts the Orchestra in a few well-known bars of 'Also Sprach Zarathustra'. He stops the Orchestra.)

CHARLEY (to audience): I'm a supermarket manager with a gold-coloured car. I know many girls because, although one is much like another, I need an outlet. I often pick them up here.

ANNA (sitting up because of GEORGE's roving hand): Stop it. (Sees CHARLEY looking at her.) Oh!

GEORGE (looking up): Would you mind leaving?

CHARLEY: Yes.

GEORGE: We want to be alone.

ANNA: We don't.

GEORGE: We do.

CHARLEY: You're bothering the lady.

GEORGE: I can't bother her. We're practically engaged.

ANNA: For goodness sake George, you do take liberties.

CHARLEY: I think you'd better go.

GEORGE: She asked me to lie down.

ANNA: To calm you.

GEORGE: When a girl asks you to lie down beside her —

CHARLEY: Do stand up.

GEORGE (turning away): I wouldn't dream of it.

ANNA (doing so): Thank you.

CHARLEY: The smell of the peat, and the shadows of the bracken, and the slow warmth seeping down from the moor – these things are very evocative, don't you think, on evenings like this?

(ANNA makes a small appreciative noise and they kiss. GEORGE turns round and sees them.)

GEORGE: How did he do that? (To CHARLEY.) Let go of that girl.

(Nothing happens but the kiss.)

That girl is mine – yes – I think so – and I don't intend to have her mauled by every passing stranger.

ANNA (from mid-kiss): Oh George.

GEORGE: If you really care for him, of course, I'll lie down in the mud and you can trample over me, but if you want the truth I'd rather kill you.

(No reaction, still kissing.)

What I'm saying, rather pointedly, is that I love you.

ANNA (mid-kiss): I treat you like dirt.

GEORGE: That's irrelevant.

CHARLEY: Go away.

GEORGE: No.

(The couple go on kissing. GEORGE is caught rather.)

I shall do something we'll all regret.

(Still there is no change.)

I think perhaps my parents dominated me too much when I was a child.

(Gaining impetus.)

I'll teach them. I shall go mad!

(He marches off. With one hand, while still kissing, CHARLEY signals to the Orchestra, who play the well-known climax to 'The Grieg Piano Concerto', and he and ANNA go off with clear intentions. Enter AMY, ALICE and ERM. AMY is free and easy. ALICE rather stringy, and ERM self-sufficient.)

AMY: So I said to him I didn't think it right.

ALICE: No.

AMY: So he said I could leave the cash register, then, and work in cold storage, and I said, 'So you can heat me up, I suppose' and he said, 'Who's bringing up interesting subjects?' and I said, 'Not me', and he said 'Can't we strike a compromise?' and he laughed so much that really I couldn't help myself because he's ever so nice, really, and his wife is like cast iron.

ALICE: Oh?

ANNA: She wears corsets and they make a lot of layers, don't they. Oh look.

(All look down over the edge of the stage.)

ANNA: A little rocky stream with pines round it.

ALICE: And somebody beside it.

> (All watch for a moment.)

AMY: They won't be troubling us, I don't imagine.

> (She moves away and spreads her arms.)

> Oh the lovely moors and the fresh wind in our faces.

> (The Orchestra begins 'Fingal's Cave'.)

ERM (to Orchestra): No thanks.

> (They stop. ERM sits. The others look about. At the side of the stage SIDNEY, a respectable and bespectacled young man, appears. He has a thermos in his pocket and carries a slab of cake.)

SIDNEY (to audience): My name's Sidney and I'm in a bus some way off and it's heading in this direction.

> (He smiles and goes off.)

ALICE: What d'you think about men, then, really.

ERM: There's kind men and there's unkind men.

AMY: You're a deep one, Erm.

ALICE: There must be more to it than that.

AMY: There are variations, but that's the basic truth.

ALICE (rather desperately): I think my Sidney must be one of the kind ones, then.

AMY: You don't want them so kind you don't notice them, Alice.

ALICE (more desperate): I know.

> (SIDNEY enters to the side of the stage again.)

SIDNEY: I'm Sidney, and I'm still on a bus and I'm getting quite near to –

> (GEORGE bursts in singing an aria in Italian of great passion, something out of Verdi, say, 'Tremenda Vendetta' from 'Rigoletto'. He stops, his head in his hand.)

SIDNEY (very slightly offended): I'm so sorry.

> (He leaves.)

ALICE: Oh, a poor mad thing storming over the heather, broken-hearted.

AMY: Careful, Alice.

ALICE: Well.

ERM: What's the matter, then.

GEORGE: Look down there. She was mine until half an hour ago.

ALICE: He is. He's broken-hearted.

GEORGE: Sometimes I think quite objectively that it wouldn't have worked, so it's better this way.

AMY: Very sensible.

GEORGE: And then my faith in my opinions disappears, and I feel so specially unhappy that I want God to reach down, pick me up, and tuck me away in a cloud.

ALICE (moved): Oh.

GEORGE: And finally I swell out, my blood goes black, and I could tear them into little bits and eat the smaller parts.

ERM: Come and sit down love.

AMY: Careful, Erm.

ALICE: Why?

AMY: He's what we call a raincoat.

ERM: I expect he wants to be understood, don't you.

GEORGE: Yes. Yes, I do. Oh yes I do.

AMY: I understand his type well enough, don't you worry.

GEORGE: I'm not a type.

AMY: Oh. Ladida.

GEORGE: Sometimes I think there could be a quality of heroism in me.

ALICE: Yes.

GEORGE: You could see me as a hero?

ALICE: Oh, I could, yes.

AMY: I think you should go out onto the moor, young man, and sing to yourself, or something, because you constitute an insult to womanhood.

GEORGE: Why?

AMY: I don't know why, but I can sense it.

GEORGE: I'm really very nice.

ERM (looking down over the stage): She's a pretty pinched looking effort, that one, if you ask me.

GEORGE: There's nothing pinched about Anna.

ERM: How do you know?

GEORGE: Because I do.

ERM: You've got too much imagination. You need some lively activity, you do.

(She leads him by the hand.)

GEORGE: Where are we going?

ERM: We're all going to get friendly behind that rock.

ALICE: Oooh, Heavens.

AMY: Not me.

ERM: Please yourself.

(She has led GEORGE off.)

AMY: I'll just come to make sure you don't get into trouble.

(She goes.)

ALICE: Me as well, Erm.

ERM (off): Yes.

ALICE (out front):
Although it may appear Sidney,
I'm turning, love, from you,
A person of this special kidney
Is something very new.

It could be that upon this hill
I'll something new discover;
Something, Sidney dear, that will
Improve you as a lover!

(She goes out. Enter SIDNEY as before.)

SIDNEY (to audience): Here I am, Sidney, still standing in my bus. I'm standing because I'm kind. You can't do much about that; either you are kind, or you aren't, and I am, and I stand a lot in buses. I'm now out of the bus, and up there are the moors. Do I see three girls and a man behind a rock? I can't be sure. But here is a rocky stream with pines and there is the gold-coloured car of the supermarket manager.

(He sits down.)

I'm here because somewhere in all this countryside is my Alice, and I would like to give her a surprise — this slab of parkin, and this thermos flask of tea. I have nice ideas like that to give my Alice little thrills of joy. It's growing cold so she'll be particularly pleased.

(He looks off.)

Evening, Charley.

ANNA (off, shocked): *Charley?*

CHARLEY (off): Like the Prince.

SIDNEY (to audience): It's also getting late.

(He draws the attention of the Orchestra.)

ANNA (off): I *am* surprised.

SIDNEY (singing with the Orchestra):
The day Thou gavest Lord is ended,
The darkness falls at thy request.
To Thee etc.

(ANNA comes in and he stops the music.)

ANNA: Is he really called Charley?

SIDNEY: Yes, and he has a wife called Pearl, and three children, and there are many other young ladies who say their life has been renewed through meeting him.

ANNA: Why does it make a difference, knowing that?

SIDNEY: Perhaps it gives him a kind of depth.

ANNA: I'm just afraid it turns him into a rather squalid experience.

SIDNEY: Oh dear. (Turns to Orchestra.) The day Thou gavest, Lord, is ended etc.

(Enter CHARLEY.)

CHARLEY: Anna!

(SIDNEY stops the Orchestra.)

CHARLEY: Has it all come as a shock?

ANNA: Yes it has.

CHARLEY: Would you like me to go?

ANNA: You don't make love like that and then waft away because you aren't who you appeared to be. There are things to be said.

(There is a little silence.)

CHARLEY: Well, for one thing, you liked it.

ANNA: I thought I did. I don't know what I think now.

(SIDNEY starts the Orchestra very quietly off on 'The day Thou Gavest', singing very quietly himself.)

For heaven's sake!

(He stops it at once.)

This is a crisis.

SIDNEY: I thought it would be soothing.

ANNA (to CHARLEY): Has anyone ever resisted you?

CHARLEY: I don't understand.

SIDNEY: Amy did, for half an hour. She told me.

CHARLEY: Oh that. Do people often resist?

ANNA: Well of course. If you'd told me you were married and your wife was called Pearl – I mean *Pearl*.

CHARLEY: You're snobbish.

ANNA: I just thought you were someone else. You pretended you were.

CHARLEY: No I didn't.

ANNA: Well, you seemed to pretend to be someone else.

SIDNEY: Would you like some parkin?

CHARLEY: Yes please.

ANNA: I wonder if you made a mistake that would've given you away if I'd noticed?

SIDNEY (breaking a bit off): I brought it out here for Alice, because it'll be getting quite chilly soon, and she does take cold easily.

CHARLEY (taking it): Sniffs a lot, doesn't she?

SIDNEY: I wouldn't say a lot.

ANNA: I can't remember any mistakes, but it's hard to think back, really.

CHARLEY (mouth full): I don't make them.

ANNA: Pardon?

CHARLEY: I don't make mistakes.

ANNA: You did give that impression, certainly.

GEORGE (off, in sepulchral tones): Anna! Can you hear me?

ANNA: Yes.

(There is a hollow laugh from GEORGE. Then his hand appears from behind a jutting-up piece of the stage. It proceeds to conduct the 'Magic Fire' music from the end of the 'Valkyrie'.)

ANNA (over music): He's on the moor. Are you all right, George?

(The hand halts the music, disappears and there is a giggle.)

SIDNEY: Perhaps he'd like some parkin.

ANNA: It's me he needs. It's me you need, isn't it George?

CHARLEY: It didn't sound like that.

ANNA: It's getting dark and I'm rather nervous. You'll have to come as well.

(She sets off.)

CHARLEY: I'd rather not, actually, it's not my thing.

ANNA (turning on him): It was your thing that put him out of his mind, so just accept responsibility for it and come with me before something awful happens.

(She goes out.)

CHARLEY (licking his fingers): They're a funny lot, aren't they. Responsibility.

SIDNEY: We'd better go, Charley. Alice, Amy and Erm are up there. Not that it was them I saw with a strange man when I arrived, it wasn't, but you can't be sure.

(They go off. Enter AMY.)

AMY (to audience): It's getting bloody chilly up here and I don't approve. Whatever it is that's going on back there, I don't approve and now it's getting dark as well.

(Enter ALICE, slowly and smiling vacantly. AMY peers towards her.)

Alice, just because she kept on coming out of that cave with a grin on her face and going back with a gurgle doesn't mean you've had everything revealed to you.

ALICE: Did you hear his voice when he shouted out?

AMY: I did. And a man who shouts another girl's name under circumstances like that hasn't had anything revealed to him at all. That Ermintrude's a funny one. Now I think of it, it was her taught me everything when I was ten behind the gasworks.

ALICE: Oh George! I wish I knew more about music.

(She conducts feebly but no music comes.)

SIDNEY (off): Alice! I've got some parkin for you!

ALICE: Oh! I can't face a lifetime of kindness, not after this. Go home Sidney.

SIDNEY (who has arrived): Poor thing. It's the exposure, I expect. Never mind, we'll have a nice warm up.

(He turns to the Orchestra and begins 'The day Thou Gavest'.)

ALICE (hands over ears): No! You mustn't. No hymn will ever reach my soul again!

(She runs out.)

SIDNEY (alarmed): She couldn't mean she's going to leave the choir.

AMY: What's that you've got? Parkin?

SIDNEY: What? Oh yes. Knowing you three girls had taken advantage of the nice weather earlier in the day to come up here for a walk, I brought some parkin and a thermos of tea as a surprise.

AMY: Bad luck, Sidney.

SIDNEY: Don't you mean thank you, Sidney?

AMY: Things have turned out differently from parkin and a thermos of tea. I think we should move off a bit and see which way they go.

SIDNEY (spirits not too high): It isn't quite what one expected, is it?

(They leave. GEORGE appears. He points at the ORCHESTRA. A wind machine makes a very loud noise and he has to bellow over it.)

GEORGE: I mean things in this world, I am significant, and people will hear me! She has released me, my faithful lover, and I will lift her far above the dross of ordinary life to the world of pure ideals and love and thought! Anna, you scorned me! You won't do that again.

(Enter ERM, who stops the wind machine.)

ERM: Go on then, do it.

(She throws him a box of matches.)

GEORGE (lighting a match): Rotheram and Sheffield, Leeds and Pontefract, Preston and Chorley, Manchester and even Wilmslow, you shall see the Pennine Chain afire from Kinderscout to Penygent.

ERM: Go on, then.

GEORGE: I'm going to.

ALICE (peering on): Go on, George.

GEORGE: Ow. (The match has burned his fingers and gone out.) Gentle Alice, there is a quality of truthfulness in you that —

ERM: Do it.

GEORGE: I will.

ERM: Now.

GEORGE: Where's Amy?

ALICE: She's gone with my poor Sid.

GEORGE: Terrified of going down to history.

ALICE: Middle class.

ERM: Get on with it.

GEORGE: Don't nag. As it happens, I feel I ought to pray before I do it.

ALICE: Oh, what a lovely man.

ERM (calm): George, set fire to this moor this minute.

GEORGE: I'll set fire to this moor when I am ultimately at one with the universe.

(He sweeps off.)

ALICE: It's all too marvellous. (Following GEORGE.) Blow winds, and tum-ti-tum your cheeks you hurricanoes.

(She's off.)

ERM (shivers, then): Sidney, you got some parkin?

(Enter AMY and CHARLEY.)

ANNA (peering): Who's that?

ERM (the same): Who's that?

ANNA: George's fiancee.

ERM: Oh well! How d'you do?

CHARLEY: Is that you, Erm?

ERM: Charley.

CHARLEY: Yes?

ERM: You with her?

CHARLEY: Yes.

ERM: What's she like?

CHARLEY: Not bad. What about him?

ERM: All right for a beginner. Sidney bring us your parkin.

ANNA: Do I understand you?

ERM: I should think so. Every ball in the wrong pocket as they say in billiards.

ANNA (shivering): It's very confusing and one feels so reduced up here.

(SIDNEY enters.)

SIDNEY: What's happening?

ERM: He's praying.

SIDNEY (pleased): Oh!

ANNA: Are you religious, too?

SIDNEY (conducting the Orchestra): The day Thou Gavest —

ERM (stopping it all): No, Sidney. He's not doing anything the Methodists would recognize.

ANNA: George? It's Anna.

(AMY appears.)

AMY: Is that you Charley?

CHARLEY: Yes.

AMY: Well give us a cuddle, I'm all goose-pimples.

SIDNEY: Is Alice there? Alice dear, it's Sidney.

GEORGE (off): You bloody fool, Alice.

SIDNEY (offended): Now *then.*

(Flames appear behind the jutting-up piece of the stage.)

GEORGE (off): You've set the whole bloody place on fire.

ALICE (scrambling up on the jutting-up piece. To Orchestra): That loud bit he had just now, please.

(The 'Magic Fire' music, loosely conducted by ALICE, comes out.)

That's it. Lovely.

CHARLEY: My goodness Alice, I must come and visit you in dairy produce some time.

AMY: She's unhealthy.

GEORGE (entering): She's set alight to the whole Pennine Chain. (To Orchestra.) Oh shut up!

(The Orchestra stops.)

ALICE (upset): George.

GEORGE: Well, look at it.

SIDNEY (suddenly running off): Never fear, Sidney's here. I'll see to it Alice.

ALICE: I don't see why you're upset. *You* were going to do it.

(GEORGE says nothing.)

ERM: Go on.

GEORGE: Go on, what?

ERM: You weren't going to do it, were you?

GEORGE: I don't think I have to answer you.

ERM (needled): Why not?

GEORGE: I suddenly find I don't much care about you.

ERM (with asperity): You weren't going to set fire to these moors and you know it.

GEORGE: I felt very urged on.

ERM: But not to that.

GEORGE: There's nothing else up here I could do but set fire to the place.

ERM: But you wouldn't have done it.

GEORGE: We don't know.

ERM: I do.

GEORGE (cross): Oh do you.

AMY: I do as well. You'd've made a mess, that's what you'd've done.

GEORGE: Oh you!

(He kicks the parkin which is lying on the ground. A piece of it goes in ANNA's eye.)

ANNA: Oh.

CHARLEY: I think you've kicked Sidney's parkin.

GEORGE: Good. They say you're a supermarket manager. Is that true, Anna?

AMY: I know your sort, young man, I said I did. You're romantic. The unkind ones always are. You couldn't be a supermarket manager if you tried.

ANNA: Yes he could be.

AMY: No he couldn't.

ANNA: Yes he could. He could do anything he wanted once he made his mind up.

AMY: That's the trouble with romantic men, they never do.

CHARLEY: I see myself as a romantic.

AMY: Oh no, you're just right, you are. The advertised thing.

(She cuddles him.)

ANNA: That's it. That's precisely what was wrong. He was totally what one hoped for, so that nothing came as a surprise.

GEORGE: Anna, d'you really think I could do whatever I wanted?

ANNA: Yes.

GEORGE: It's going very cold, suddenly.

ALICE: Well no wonder. Sidney's quenched the burning mountain with his thermos flask of tea. No one asked you to, Sidney.

SIDNEY (entering): Since the weather forecast said it was going to turn nasty, I made this flask of tea to warm you girls up. As it happens, I was able to cool you down! Where's the parkin?

ANNA: George kicked it.

GEORGE: Can we go now?

SIDNEY: Why did you do that?

GEORGE: It was only parkin.

SIDNEY (hurt): It was mine. There's no need to kick people's parkin all over the moors. Yes, I think we should go.

ERM: Ask her to marry you.

GEORGE: Here?

ERM: It's up to you, George.

GEORGE: Will you marry me, Anna?

ANNA: Yes, of course I will, thank you.

GEORGE: That's that settled. Are you going to stay up there all night?

ALICE (to whom this was addressed): Oh George.

SIDNEY: Come along, Alice. You always catch cold if you cry.

CHARLEY: We can all go home in my car if you like.

GEORGE: Thank you, but Anna and I will find our way home. There are things which have to be said, and we probably won't be home until the dawn.

ANNA: But it's so cold.

GEORGE (leading her off): The sooner we get home to have some soup, the better. Fortunately I've another slab of parkin in the larder.

ERM (now alone, to audience): And so everybody lived happily ever after. Charley had his supermarket, and everything, Sidney had his Alice, more or less, and George became a psychiatric social worker, a job which Anna came to understand and admire, once she overcame her prejudices. As for me, I'm a fairy godmother, and they always end up on their own. Good night.

(She goes off.)

END

The Problem

THE PROBLEM was first presented by the Midlands Arts Centre Repertory Company at the Studio Theatre, Birmingham, on 11 December 1970 with the following cast:

MAN   *Rhys McConnochie*
A CRAB

Directed by Philip Hedley

A MAN in a bathing costume stands with a towel round his shoulders. He is being brave for clearly he is in pain and clearly he is trying to hide it. After a moment or two he lifts his right foot to show the audience that a CRAB is biting his toe and will not let go. He puts his foot down again very gingerly.

MAN: As the French would say, impasse. I'm a vegetarian, I cannot take life.

(He stares at the CRAB. Suddenly he shouts at it.)

I cannot take life! Let go!

(Nothing from the CRAB. To audience.)

Bloody crustaceans. Man is superior, you see. I have made some advance over simple animal instincts with regard to food.

(To CRAB.)

I couldn't eat you. I couldn't eat *you*. So why the hell don't you follow my example?

(To audience.)

There are times — really — there are times when one thinks they deserve everything they get. Not that it's entirely their fault. They're thick, that's all, thick.

(To CRAB, shouting.)

Thick, bloody thick, thick as two short planks.

(He suddenly howls in pain, as if the CRAB has just bitten harder. Then to audience.)

He knows. If I could have the R.S.P.C.A. here — ha! — What an eye-opener.

(To CRAB.)

I'll say it all again then, after which, if you please, we'll try to agree on something. I am a man. I could kill you. I could cook you, I could eat you. Yet, although I have the teeth of a carnivore, a howling need for high protein food, and a history based on my ability to kill, I have disciplined myself. I have accepted an artificial law — all laws are artificial — all *man's* laws are artificial, because artifice is the special thing about man — you don't go in for artifice — well, there's bird's nests, but they don't apply to you, you as a crab — the point is, I have accepted as the most civilized artificial law I can think of the total renunciation of these three things − a) my carnivorous teeth; b) my high protein diet; and c) my accursed history of murder. Please tweak me if you understand so far.

(He howls in response to a tweak. To audience.)

They're not so green as they're cabbage looking, you know.

(To CRAB.)

Now listen, I have made a society which allows me to practise these laws. Dentists look after my teeth, cheese provides my high protein diet, and Christo-Platonism has taught me that loving my neighbour is a more econo-mical and indeed more sympathetic approach to him than murder. These are the triumphs of man, Homo Sapiens, the Thinker. We have a statue of him in our world, a rather slow-witted figure, actually, but athletic, contemplating more or less the place where his shoe laces would be if he weren't stark naked. (He is slightly puzzled by remembering the Thinker.) The Thinker. Yes. Well, the Thinker is man created in his own image by man. (Smiles.) We can do anything. In this case, for example, I have made certain advances, or, depending on your position, have accepted certain limitations, that will spare you your life in a situation where normally you would be killed. Oh what a noble creature I am. How I have advanced myself towards Heaven! What I now ask of you, oh crab, is that you make the same advance towards Heaven, just for two seconds, so that I can go home to tea. What about it?

(He gives a long howl of pain. Then to Heaven.)

I have tried. (To audience.) I've been here longer than you (To heaven.) − Haven't I − (To audience.) going through it with him, showing him the light. (To Heaven.) Your light, my light, everybody's light. Men and Gods witness! It is not my fault! I cannot put my clothes on below the waist while this crab holds my foot, and if he bites any harder I might die of septicaemia or loss of blood.

(To CRAB.)

That is how it is between us, and that is what is forcing me to consider being realistic.

(He reveals a stone he has been holding in his hands under the towel. He reveals it to the audience and smiles diabolically.)

Draconian measures. (To CRAB.) I shall drop this on your back if you don't let go.

(Nothing from the CRAB.)

I shall count three. One, two, three. Goodbye, crab.

(He smashes the CRAB. A great female howl arises from the unhappy CRAB. The man looks quite stunned. Then, the howl continuing, he manages to get away, now free, to a pile of clothes. He sits and puts on a sock. He looks back worried at the CRAB. It stops howling. In the silence he makes a slight move towards it. Then −)

CRAB (in pain): Oh bloody hell.

MAN (relieved that it can talk): Ah. Yes. Now you know what it feels like.

CRAB: Bloody, bloody hell.

MAN (reaching for the other sock): I'm sorry, but you were given a number of chances.

CRAB: I'm dying. Bloody hell, I'm dying.

MAN: Yes. Well, you'll realize I'm very sorry about that, feeling the way I do. (The CRAB whimpers piteously.) Quiet. (Looks to Heaven.) Make it quiet. (Feels the presence of the audience.) I did try to explain. (To CRAB.) I tried to explain.

CRAB: I didn't understand.

MAN: Oh, now — come.

CRAB: I didn't understand.

MAN (looks to Heaven as if checking whether this is possible. Then to CRAB): What didn't you understand?

CRAB: I didn't understand anything.

MAN: Well you should've tried! (He looks to Heaven.) Why didn't *You* make it understand? Tongues of fire and all that? (To audience.) I tried. (To CRAB.) Are you still alive?

CRAB (slowly dying): I didn't understand.

MAN: Well don't die and I'll tell you again. Crab? Don't die. After this experience you'll realize what I mean. Crab? (He kneels by the CRAB.)

CRAB (more quietly): I didn't understand.

MAN: Don't die. Crab? (He lies on his tummy and speaks quietly.) Crab! I'll try again.

CRAB (faint whisper): I didn't understand.

MAN: Crab, I'll try again.

CRAB (very faint): I didn't understand.

MAN: Crab? Crab! I'll try again, crab. Crab?

END

Jack in the Box

A Brief Essay in Science Fiction

JACK IN THE BOX was first performed by the Midlands Arts Centre Repertory Company at the Studio Theatre, Birmingham, on 26 March 1971 with the following cast:

HILBOURNE	*Neil McLauchlan*
JACK	*John Hug*

ASSISTANTS   *Jane Briers*
                                    Martin Duncan

Directed by Philip Hedley

Enter HILBOURNE.

HILBOURNE: Right. (To off.) Right?

SOMEONE OFF: Right!

HILBOURNE (to audience): Once upon a time there was this man who thought of something in his bath. I know exactly how he felt.

(Some ASSISTANTS carry on a huge box. HILBOURNE looks at it with love, but dispassionately.)

Mine. Eureka. I won't go through the farce of asking for a volunteer because I won't risk the relatives complaining. Jack will do it. Jack's done everything. Good old Jack.

(Suddenly silent reflection. Enter JACK. He waits. He coughs.)

HILBOURNE (surprised in his reflection): Oh! In you go then.

(JACK goes toward the box.)

HILBOURNE (quietly): Jack?

JACK: Yes.

HILBOURNE (concerned): You all right?

JACK: Don't worry. Just don't worry.

(JACK gets into box.)

HILBOURNE: Right.

(Suddenly he turns to the audience and, hugging himself, bursts into song and dance. The ASSISTANTS join him, and they all dance in great excitement and pleasure.)

ALL (sing): I'm a clever man, I'm a clever man,
I'm a clever, clever, clever man.
I'm a clever man, I'm a clever man,
I'm a clever, clever, clever man.

(After a time or two through, HILBOURNE halts, with a dreadful thought. HILBOURNE sings in a slow holy manner, looking up.)

I only hope it works,
With all my heart and soul.
Please make sure it works
Oh please make sure it works.

(The ASSISTANTS join in with fervour and it goes through a time or two.)

JACK (interrupting. He is in the box): Ready.

HILBOURNE: O.K. then.

JACK: O.K.

HILBOURNE (presses a knob): O.K.

(All wait. HILBOURNE holds stop-watch.)

JACK (after a while): Metabolic rate altering. (Then.) Feathers beginning to sprout about the coccyx.

HILBOURNE: The feet should go. Right?

JACK: Right. Claw at the rear a bit painful. (Pause.) O.K. now.

HILBOURNE: Breast feathers will take a minute. (To audience. Quite conceited.) My name is Hilbourne. I'm demonstrating the last in a series of experiments in metamorphosis. Jack is turning into a bird. (He turns back.) Any reduction in size?

JACK: No.

HILBOURNE: None?

JACK: Breast feathers nearly through.

HILBOURNE: And no reduction in size?

JACK: No.

HILBOURNE: Oh.

(There is a rustling and swooshing sound, as of a large bird in a box.)

JACK: It's getting a bit stuffy, actually.

(The swooshing goes on.)

Hilbourne? I — I think something's a bit wrong.

HILBOURNE: No.

JACK: Then why aren't I going down? Hilbourne? Hilbourne!

(A desperate clawing sound. Then a choking sound that turns into the awful kind of cawing noise a peacock makes.)

HILBOURNE (a bit cross): Jack! (Silence.) Are you laying an egg?

(Cawing breaks out again, pitiful and threatening.)

ASSISTANT: The box is cracking here.

(It is.)

HILBOURNE: Jack, are you fucking the whole thing up?

(The box collapses and a huge, horrid, unfunny bird is revealed. It shouts and screams in a nervous way, and makes attempts to move, clumsily. It caws horribly.)

Don't make that ridiculous noise at me!

(It turns and is silent.)

You're supposed to be a canary. Look at you. When I picked you out from all the other laboratory assistants to give you immortality as a bird man, I did so because I thought you worthy of that honour. You were prepared to work yourself into the ground. You never questioned me, because I was right wasn't I, because I am right, because it's you, you Jack, who have interfered with your metabolic adjustments and made a balls-up of it. A balls-up of my whole life.

(Cawing.)

Shut your filthy noise.

ASSISTANT: It's Jack.

HILBOURNE: It is not!

(Silence.)

Yes of course it is. Of course it's Jack. Take him away please.

ASSISTANT: What should —

HILBOURNE: Ring his neck. (To audience.) Now you can all enjoy hating me because I don't feel guilty. (Going out.) Anyone can take him home for a pet of course.

(Fade on revolting cawing.)

END

SONG for JACK IN THE BOX

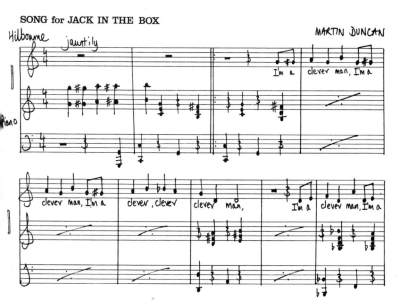

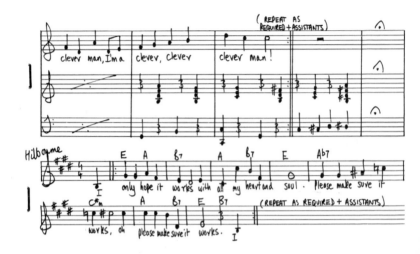

If You Don't Laugh You Cry

IF YOU DON'T LAUGH YOU CRY was first presented by the Midlands Arts Centre Repertory Company at the Studio Theatre, Birmingham, on 26 March 1971 with the following cast:

HITLER   *Barry McGinn*
COMIC   *Jane Briers*

Directed by Philip Hedley

Lights up on HITLER with trombone. 'Tannhauser' playing. HITLER raises trombone to join in. Enter COMIC.

COMIC: Hello, Hello, Hello. (Silence.) How many letters are there in the alphabet? (Answering herself.) How many letters are there in the alphabet? There are 26 letters in the alphabet. No, there are 23 letters in the alphabet because you and I aren't there and the angel said Noel.

(Silence. HITLER starts playing again but is stopped.)

Hold on, hold on, hold on. Here's another one. This gamekeeper went out hunting for game. He saw this girl and she had nothing on and he said, 'Are you game?' and she said 'Yes' so he shot her.

(HITLER starts playing.)

I say, I say, I say. A little demonstration.

(HITLER stops playing.)

Hold up the index and little fingers of your right hand. The index and little fingers of your right hand? Yes, the index and little fingers of your right hand.

(HITLER does it.)

Thank you. Now, say 'wing, wing, wing, wing'.

(HITLER silently mouths this. THE COMIC seizes on the imaginary telephone from between his fingers):

Hello. Pwimwose, thwee four, thwee five.

(After a moment HITLER plays.)

Wait!

(Silence.)

What is the difference between a letter box and an elephant's bottom?

(HITLER starts playing.)

(Through the music.) I wouldn't send you to post a letter. I said, I wouldn't send you to post a letter.

(HITLER stops and stares at her.)

(Stares back and says —) There was an old woman who lived in a shoe. She had so many children she didn't know what to do — apparently.

(HITLER — no reaction.)

What comes out of cows with a splash? The royal yacht.

(HITLER — no reaction.)

Cowes is a place in the Isle of Wight. Splash. Cowes. There were two men and a girl on a desert island. After a week the girl was so ashamed she killed herself. After another week, the men were so ashamed, they buried her. After another week, the men were so ashamed —

(HITLER begins to play loud final section of 'Tannhauser'.)

(Following on.) — they dug her up again. Did you hear about the Eskimo couple who got engaged one winter? It grew so cold they broke it off. Then there was the brush who said to the other brush, 'I'm going to have a little bristle' and the other brush said, 'Impossible. We haven't swept together'. 'Good heavens' said the boy strawberry to the girl strawberry, 'How did we get in this jam?'. 'Because we were both found in the same bed.' 'Tell me, Edward', said Queen Alexandra on her wedding night, 'Do the poor do this?' 'Yes, my dear,' said Edward. 'Well stop them, it's too good.' There was this man who said he could fart a solo part in a Mozart concerto, so he was hired to do it at the Albert Hall. Just as the orchestra was about to play, he shat on the stage. 'Good heavens' said Sir Thomas Beecham. 'What are you doing?' 'Clearing my throat, of course.' And what about the manure in Noah's Ark? They saved it up for ages and shovelled it overboard. Four thousand years later, Columbus discovered it. There was this chambermaid in Scotland went to bed —

(HITLER, still playing, catches her in the kidneys with the trombone.)

— went to bed with a travelling salesman.

(HITLER swipes her with the trombone.)

(Totters.) As she got undressed —

(HITLER knocks her to the floor.)

— she began to whistle.

(HITLER hits her in the stomach with the trombone.)

(Faintly.) The salesman kicked her out, saying —

(HITLER prods her hard again.)

(Silence.)

(Faintly.) 'I'll no sleep with anyone who whistles on Sabbath.'

(HITLER gives her another vicious jab. HITLER smiles. Stands on the COMIC and through the final chords 'Sieg Heil's' and then opens his arms to heaven. The lights fade.)

END